What's My Why

Do you want to be happier and help the people around you be happier too? That's my why! My name is Julie Radlauer, and I am a Doctor of Public Health and a licensed mental health counselor. This combination of education and experience has allowed me to focus my energies on the prevention of diagnosable mental health conditions. My area of expertise is on the social influences of mental health. And I bring research to life to arm everyday people with the tools necessary to improve their own mental health and support others. I break down difficult concepts into tangible techniques that we can all use, every day, to lean in and support others. I have worked with individuals, organizations, systems, and communities to share these practices over the years, and now I am excited to share them with you.

There are so many people struggling these days, and I believe that if we just focus on the social influences of mental health, we can improve the lives of ourselves and those around us. We each have the power to take control over our individual mental health. Further, collectively, we can support each other to address the social influences and lift each other up.

My mission is to change the narrative on the treatment of mental health conditions. Please join me in this movement- collectively through our understanding of social connections, social support, social capital, social media, and social inclusion, we can all experience positive mental health and wellbeing.

Julie Radlauer, DrPH, LMHC
CEO, Collectively

For more information on the social influences
of mental health watch my TED Talk:

collective

Who is Collectively

Collectively strives to advance mental well-being by engaging diverse advocates, supporters, and decision-makers to collectively solve complex challenges. We address mental well-being through a variety of approaches to create change, including the collective process of a community of support, capacity building, and the development and expansion of social capital. Services and supports are provided at the individual, organizational, system, and community levels. Collectively centers on:

Collaboration: We believe that all challenges can be solved when the right people are sitting at the table

Individuality: We believe that mental well-being cannot be addressed in the same way for every person. We honor the diversity and experiences of all people

Impact: We believe that mental wellness should be addressed at the individual, organizational, community, and global levels

Innovation: We believe that addressing the ever-changing needs for mental well-being requires innovative ways of thinking and acting

Connection: We believe that mental well-being comes from support, community, and a sense of belonging created through a collective process

Acknowledgements

This book would not be possible without the support of some very special organizations and individuals. I am incredibly grateful to Southeast Florida Behavioral Health Network for their ongoing partnership and sponsorship on this project. Additionally, I would like to thank Claudia Evangelista for her research expertise and organizational skills in pulling this initiative together. I am also appreciative of Jona Bacolod for her ongoing commitment to the process of getting information about the social influences of mental health out into the universe to support changing the narrative of mental health. Finally, this book would not be what it is without the design expertise of Brent Clemens, thank you for your patience and sharing your talent with the world.

Introduction

According to the World Health Organization (WHO), we are experiencing a global mental health crisis with over 1 billion people struggling with their mental health. Further, what if I told you that 1 in 3 people are struggling with loneliness? This is a problem because loneliness is the greatest indicator of depression. Unfortunately, with numbers like these, there are not nearly enough mental health professionals to meet the need. Sounds like a recipe for disaster, right?!? Well, the good news is that for many of these people, they can get their mental health needs met outside of the professional mental health setting. In fact, research out of Harvard University estimates that 80% of people experiencing mental health symptoms can have their needs met through less formal treatment options.

So, what are these less formal mental health options you ask? Well, in this book we are going to use science to help you meet your mental health needs. There is extensive research about how your everyday actions contribute to your mental health. The intention is to educate you about how you can actually take control of your mental health, before it gets to a crisis space. This book is going to focus on the Social Influences of Mental Health. By understanding how social aspects of our lives impact our happiness and wellbeing, we can begin to incorporate everyday strategies into our daily practice.

What, you don't believe me? Well, just think about this for a moment, have you ever been in a really bad mood, maybe you were even crying. If in that moment, a friend or family member leaned in and offered words of encouragement, a supportive hug, or even a funny joke, didn't you begin to feel a little better? Research around some of the social influences like social connections and social support corroborate this story. When we have documented support in our lives, we experience better mental and physical health outcomes, in fact we actually live 3.67 years longer when we have strong social connections. The goal is to harness these social influences to create the support that we need on a regular basis. By intentionally practicing to manage the social influences in your life, you can create the balance that you need to be happier and healthier. The good news is that most of these techniques are fun and easy to incorporate into your life.

"Man is by nature a social animal."

–Aristotle

What the Research Says About Mental Health

There is extensive research about how human beings are social creatures. According to Michael Platt, a biological anthropologist from University of Pennsylvania's Perelman School of Medicine, "This social behavior is a critical part of our adaptive toolkit. It allows us to come together and do things that we wouldn't be able to do on our own." In fact, our drive to connect with others is embedded in our biology and evolutionary history. Scientists believe we are essentially wired to connect with other people because natural selection favors humans and of our ability to care for our children and organize into groups. So, scientifically we know that social aspects of our life have benefitted us historically, what about in the present day?

Current research on the benefits of the social influences in our lives demonstrates that when we embrace the social aspect, we see both mental and physical benefits. In fact, did you know that socially connected people:

- Have an increased life span by 3.67 years

- Experience less stress

- Have better cardiovascular health and reduced risk of death from cardiovascular disease

- Have better immune systems

- Are less likely to have mental health conditions (including depression and anxiety)

- Are less likely to experience dementia and Alzheimer's

- Being socially connected actually helps you think faster

And these are just a few of the documented benefits of the social influences on your mental and physical health.

These social aspects can be considered protective factors, and the better your protective factors, the easier it is for you to address some of the negative things that are happening around you. Our purpose with this book is to help you understand why you should intentionally incorporate these aspects into your life, and then once you understand the why behind the benefits, then we can talk about the how.

So, let's learn about what I like to call the Social Influences of Mental Health addressed in this book. We are going to focus on the following social aspects that can be incorporated into our lives in meaningful and productive ways.

Social Connections- Socially connected people experience a sense of belonging to a group and feel close to other people (Berkeley University). Further, social connection is "the energy that exists between people when they feel seen, heard, and valued; when they can give and receive without judgement, and when they derive sustenance and strength from the relationship". (Brene Brown). Being socially connected is the experience of feeling close and connected to others. It involves feeling loved, cared for, and valued, and forms the basis of our interpersonal relationships. Having social connections in your life has been documented to improve your mental health.

Social Support- The help, advice, and comfort that we receive from those with whom we have stable, positive relationships defines social support. It includes supportive relationships and access to social networks comprised of the following functions: emotional, tangible, informational, and companionship support. Social support can either be actual or perceived support and includes reciprocity, mutuality, and equality. When you have social support you can get through difficult challenges, resulting in better mental health.

Social Capital- The structure of networks and collective resources within a community that individuals within that community can draw upon and that will benefit them. Social capital refers to the relationships among people who live and work in a particular society, enabling that society to function effectively. This sense of community connection and belonging derived from social capital positively influences mental health.

Social Media- There are demonstrated connections between social media and mental health. Technically, the definition of social media includes the websites and applications that enable users to create and share content or to participate in social networking. And, because social media is so widely used, it is necessary to understand how to use this connection tool in a way that will promote better mental health individually and collectively.

Social Inclusion- Social inclusion is when all groups of people have the same rights, opportunities, access to resources, and benefits. Addressing social inclusion acknowledges that historical inequalities exist and must be remedied through specific measures, with a recognition that this process should be participatory, collaborative, inclusive of difference, and affirming of personal agency. Focusing efforts to understand, advocate for, and commit to creating an equitable society improves both individual, and ultimately, collective mental health.

Collectively's Approach to the Social Influence of Mental Health

In order to experience benefit in each of the above-mentioned disciplines of the Social Influences of mental health, let's practice utilizing science-based elements of connection and support. The elements below have been identified through research as contributing factors to successful connection and the promotion of mental health and wellbeing.

Intentionality- It takes energy and thought to create connection. Like anything in life, when we put our attention towards something we can create impact. Creating connections and supports takes work.

Proximity (if possible)- The principle of proximity states that physical and psychological nearness to others tends to increase interpersonal liking. In essence, people are more likely to form social relationships with people that are closer in proximity to them.

Connectivity- The energy that exists between people when they spend time together and share experiences. True connection requires presence and a degree of mutual dependence from the relationship.

Commonality- When individuals have shared interests and purpose with others there is a natural connection. This connection creates an opportunity for bonding and potential future support.

Vulnerability- Making authentic connections requires uncertainty, risk, transparency, and emotional exposure. Taking that first step to connect with others and truly be who you are potentially results in building connections and support systems.

Dependability- An important aspect of support is that people are "there for you" when truly needed. This includes on a consistent basis as well as in times of need. Rituals, traditions, and scheduled activities create the opportunity for accountability.

Reciprocity- the practice of exchanging things with others for mutual benefit. We feel connected to others when they will help us as well as allow us to help them in times of need. Reciprocal relationships result in sustainable support.

Flexibility- One of the biggest challenges in making connections and building supports is that we have expectations for when and how others should act. When we practice unconditional regard for others and generosity of spirit, this allows us to alter our expectations and meet people where they are, thus creating an opportunity for connection.

Positivity- This does not only relate to people having a positive attitude, though that certainly helps. The element of positivity relates to valuing an existing relationship, feeling cared for, and knowing you are accepted.

About this Book

This book is designed to share research, tangible tools, and simple techniques about the Social Influences of Mental Health.

For many of us, when we have an intentional focus on learning about, expanding and utilizing these social influences on a regular basis, we are creating the buffer that we need to steer clear of mental health symptoms. In this book we are going to learn about each of the social influences of mental health. We will share research about why addressing this aspect of your life will improve your mental health. Additionally, tangible tools and techniques are shared through the activities presented. When these activities are utilized and practiced, you will see the benefits of the social influences. The goal is to become comfortable utilizing these practices in our daily life. The more we intentionally lean on the social influences, the greater likelihood that we will live a happier, healthier life.

Some of the activities shared in this workbook are for you on the individual level. Additionally, we are sharing some activities that should be completed with another person in order to achieve maximum benefit. We are also sharing some group activities that can be practiced in small groups. We encourage you to intentionally focus your efforts on the social influences of mental health to build social connections, social support, and social capital in your life. Additionally, understanding social media and how it can both positively and negatively impact your life will help you make informed decisions that will improve your mental health. Lastly, in today's world, we must all strive to understand how the inclusion in society needs to be addressed in order to improve collective mental well-being.

This book is designed to provide you with tangible tools and techniques that you can use to embrace the social influences of mental health. Make time to read and reflect, grab your journal, or pull together friends or family to talk through what you are about the read. We can all use the activities shared in this book to take stock of and expand the social influences in our lives. We are excited to share this science with you in hopes that collectively, we will harness the social influences to improve our mental health.

Contents

collectively

We will start with an assessment of the Social Influences of Mental Health. Please take the time to complete the assessment tool on the following pages and identify which aspects of the social influences of mental health you need to focus on to improve your life.

The Social Influences of Mental Health (SIMH) are based in science and there is extensive research that each of these social aspects of our lives impacts our level of happiness. Use this assessment to identify how the SIMH are impacting your life today.

SOCIAL CONNECTIONS:

Social connection is "the energy that exists between people when they feel seen, heard, and valued; when they can give and receive without judgement, and when they derive sustenance and strength from the relationship".

Being socially connected is the experience of feeling close and connected to others. It involves feeling loved, cared for, and valued, and forms the basis of our interpersonal relationships.

Rate the connection in your life. Answer the questions below:

	Not at all	A little	Most of the time	All the time
I have someone in my life who doesn't judge me	1	2	3	4
I have someone in my life who shows me love and affection	1	2	3	4
I have someone in my life who is proud of me	1	2	3	4
I have someone in my life who stands by me during hard times	1	2	3	4
I have someone in my life who has the same interests and we spend time together	1	2	3	4

How many different people did you identify when answering these questions? _____

If you were able to identify at least three different people and you are satisfied with your answers above, you do not need to focus on this area of social influence. If you were not able to identify at least three different people, or you answered a 1 or 2 to some of the questions above, this is a potential social influence that you should focus on.

Identify what social connections you would like to bring into your life.

_____

_____

SOCIAL SUPPORT:

The help, advice, and comfort that we receive from those with whom you have stable, positive relationships defines social support. It includes supportive relationships and access to social networks comprised of the following functions: emotional, tangible, informational, and companionship support. Social support can either be actual or perceived support and includes reciprocity, mutuality, and equality.

Rate the following support in your life. Answer the questions below:

	Not at all	A little	Most of the time	All the time
Someone will make a meal for me if I'm not feeling well	1	2	3	4
Someone will give me sound advice in a time of crisis	1	2	3	4
I have someone to celebrate holidays and special events with	1	2	3	4
I have someone to have a good time with	1	2	3	4
Someone will show up for me if I truly need support	1	2	3	4

How many different people did you identify when answering these questions? _____

If you were able to identify at least three different people and you are satisfied with your answers above, you do not need to focus on this area of social influence. If you were not able to identify at least three different people, or you answered a 1 or 2 to some of the questions above, this is a potential social influence that you should focus on.

Identify what social support you would like to bring into your life.

_____

_____

SOCIAL CAPITAL:

By definition, social capital is the structure of networks and collective resources within a community that individuals within that community can draw upon and that will benefit them. Social capital refers to the relationships among people who live and work in a particular society, enabling that society to function effectively.

Answer the questions below:

	Not at all	A little	Most of the time	All the time
I have someone in my life that I look up to/ guides me	1	2	3	4
I have someone in my life that will connect me to resources	1	2	3	4
I am a valued member of a group that meets regularly	1	2	3	4
I am a member of a faith/spiritual community	1	2	3	4
I am open to receiving support and will actively give support to others	1	2	3	4

How many different people/groups did you identify when answering these questions? _____

If you were able to identify at least three different people/groups and you are satisfied with your answers above, you do not need to focus on this area of social influence. If you were not able to identify at least three different people/groups, or you answered a 1 or 2 to some of the questions above, this is a potential social influence that you should focus on.

Identify what social capital you would like to bring into your life.

_____

_____

SOCIAL MEDIA:

The definition of social media includes the websites and applications that enable users to create and share content or to participate in social networking. Let's be clear, there are both positive and negative aspects of social media, and social media is a communication tool that is here to stay. Understanding how you use social media is important.

Answer the questions below:

	Not at all	A little	Most of the time	All the time
I engage others on social media with positive comments	1	2	3	4
I am able to walk away from social media without trouble	1	2	3	4
I spend less than 2 hours on social media daily	1	2	3	4
I am able to separate emotionally from what I see on social media – it does not impact me	1	2	3	4
I use social media to schedule time to connect with others in person	1	2	3	4

If you were satisfied with your answers above, you do not need to focus on this area of social influence. If you answered a 1 or 2 to some of the questions above, this is a potential social influence that you should focus on.

Identify what you want to change about your relationship with social media.

_____

_____

SOCIAL INCLUSION:

Social inclusion is when all groups of people have the same rights, opportunities, access to resources, and benefits. Addressing social inclusion acknowledges that historical inequalities exist and must be remedied through specific measures, with a recognition that this process should be participatory, collaborative, inclusive of difference, and affirming of personal agency. Focusing efforts to understand, advocate for, and commit to creating an equitable society improves both individual, and ultimately, collective mental health.

Answer the questions below:

	Not at all	A little	Most of the time	All the time
I do things to make the world a better place, even if it does not directly impact me	1	2	3	4
When an opportunity arises, I advocate for fairness for all	1	2	3	4
I learn about differences, so I understand other's experiences	1	2	3	4
I participate with friends/family in activities to promote equity	1	2	3	4
I am aware of the access that I have, and I support others if they don't have the same access	1	2	3	4

If you are satisfied with your answers above, you do not need to focus on this area of social influence. If you answered a 1 or 2 to some of the questions above, this is a potential social influence that you should focus on.

Identify how you would like to incorporate social inclusion into your life differently.

By understanding how each of these social aspects of our lives impacts our mental health, you can begin to see the path forward. It's important to take an audit of your life to understand your current situation (baseline) and then identify what changes need to be made in order to benefit fully from each of the influences. You want to take an honest look at each influence and ask how satisfied you are in this space. Further when we learn how to intentionally incorporate specific interventions into our lives in meaningful and productive ways, our mental health improves. So, use this tool to learn about the five social influences and the best ways to use them to meet our mental health needs.

"There comes a point where we need to stop pulling people out of the river. We need to go upstream and find out why they're falling in."

–Archbishop Desmond Tutu

Chapter 1 ~ Social Connections

According to Harvard University, forty-three percent of young adults reported increases in loneliness since the outbreak of the pandemic. Further, the CDC reports that sixty-one percent of young adults reported feeling serious loneliness in the prior month, compared to twenty-four percent of survey respondents aged 55-65. This statistic should be appalling, as our young people are almost three times as lonely as mid-aged adults! The proposed reason for this rise in loneliness is lack of social connection with peers resulting in poor mental health.

University of Chicago researcher John Cacioppo identifies loneliness as the absence of meaningful social interaction such as an intimate relationship, friendships, family gatherings, or even community. We know that humans are a social species, and we derive strength from our collective ability to communicate and work together. Research demonstrates that we need human connection, and connecting with others on a physical and emotional level improves our health and overall well-being. Sadly, statistics demonstrate that many of us are not making those human connections in a way to support their overall mental health and well-being.

Even before the COVID-19 pandemic, mental health challenges were the leading cause of disability and poor life outcomes in young people, with up to 1 in 5 children ages 3 to 17 in the US with a reported mental, emotional, developmental, or behavioral disorder. In 2016, of the 7.7 million children with treatable mental health disorders, about half did not receive the treatment they needed. There are many barriers to people accessing mental health support including; cultural beliefs, access to services, capacity of the behavioral health system to meet the need, financial limitations, stigma, and the list goes on and on. When people experience mental health crises and do not seek support, their conditions deteriorate.

Unfortunately, in recent years, national surveys of youth have shown major increases in certain mental health symptoms, including depressive symptoms and suicidal ideation. Here are some alarming facts:

- Between 2009 to 2019, the proportion of high school students reporting persistent feelings of sadness or hopelessness increased by 40%.

- The number seriously considering attempting suicide increased by 36%.

- Those reported to create a suicide plan increased by 44%.

- Between 2011 and 2015, youth psychiatric visits to emergency departments for depression, anxiety, and behavioral challenges increased by 28%.

- Between 2007 and 2018, suicide rates among youth ages 10-24 in the US increased by 57%.

- The National Center for Health Statistics suggests there were tragically more than 6,600 deaths by suicide among the 10-24 age group in 2020.

While some experts believe that the trends in reporting of mental health challenges are partly due to young people becoming more willing to openly discuss mental health concerns, other researchers point to the growing use of social media, academic pressure, lack of access to mental health support, substance use, and stressors such as societal factors including financial challenges, rising income inequality, racism, gun violence, and climate change.

Sadly, the above examples of societal happenings in the world are a source of stress for many, resulting in mental health symptoms. What we do know is that in a time of crisis, an all hands on deck approach is required. While you may be thinking to yourself, "How can I possible solve this problem?" I am here to tell you that we can all impact the mental health of others. You don't need to be an expert in mental health treatment, nor do you need to have a special degree in counseling. In order to support our own mental health and the mental health of those around us, we need to start by focusing on building connections.

In Zimbabwe, there's a program that focuses on connection called the Friendship Bench. This intervention is comprised of a group of grandmothers who were trained in brief mental health interventions and strategically placed outside of health clinics. While people wait in line to see the doctor, they can join the elderly women on the bench just to talk and get support. So, is this intervention going to treat a person suffering with major depression? Of course not, but according to Harvard, 80% of people struggling with mental health conditions can have their needs met outside of the clinical care setting through something called community-based care. Friendship Benches are a great example of community-based care and for 80% of the people; this brief intervention is going to help meet their needs. Just this brief experience of connection with another person improves mental health symptoms.

When we focus on social connections, we can quickly see how we can all support each other in times of need. So, what are the benefits of social connection you ask?

According to the Center for the Study of Social Policy, social connection is considered a protective factor and having social connection is a buffer against stress. So, when we are exposed to stressful experiences, being connected with friends and family can actually protect us from the harmful effects of stress on our mental health.

An important component of understanding social connectedness is that it is "subjective" and based upon an individual's perception of connection. This means that a person's perception of their social connectedness may not necessarily be the reality. Sometimes, we are surrounded by others, yet feel lonely, or we can be isolated from others, but still feel connected.

For many people making connections is difficult, it requires us to be vulnerable and open. But understanding that the benefits outweigh the risks in many circumstances, it is important to take the leap. For me, when I understand why I need to do something that makes me uncomfortable, I am more willing to give it a try. The science around the benefits of connection says I will live longer, be happier, be physically healthier, and even think faster when I have connections in my life.

Once I understand the why and embrace it, it's helpful for me to know what is actually involved, like what do I have to do in order to achieve connection. This conceptual framework of social connectedness is really helpful to understand the components of connection. Here are five dimensions identified that describe the experience of social connectedness:

- **Closeness**: the degree of mutual dependence between two people

- **Identity and common bond**: believing one shares important characteristics with other people

- **Valued relationships**: valuing and/or positively appraising an existing relationship

- **Involvement**: perceived level of involvement and social engagement with others, including group/network involvement and companionship

- **Cared for and accepted**: feeling that one is cared for, including social acceptance and social support

So, that doesn't seem so difficult, right? If we look for others that share our interests, lean on them and show up for them when they need us, we are on our way. Further, supporting others through connection also lifts us up and improves our mental health. Science on altruism demonstrates that when we do something nice for others, we also experience the benefits. Creating opportunities where every day people can lean in and support each other through connections is a win-win.

This chapter is designed to provide you with opportunities to explore ways to expand your connections. On the following pages there are activities that can be done individually, in pairs with a friend, on even in small groups of people. These activities prompt you to look at yourself and your connections. Be honest, take the time to think through how you want to expand your horizons, remember that we can never have too many connections in this world.

Following are some activities you may use to assess, identify, build, and cultivate your support systems.

The Science around connections says:

- it takes 50 hours to turn an acquaintance into a casual friend,

- 90 hours to move from casual friend to friend,

- more than 200 hours to qualify as a best friend.

Also, we usually are closest to no more than 5 people, call about 15 people our friends, and our brain can only hold about 150 people as meaningful relationships.

"Courage is not having the strength to go on, it is going on when you don't have the strength."

–T Roosevelt

Activity 1: Social Connection Survey

Goal: To take an inventory of your social connections

Let's start with a personal inventory of your social connections. Answer honestly and instinctively. You don't have to share these results with anyone. This is a helpful way to look at the social connections in your life and may help with providing ideas for improving your social connections. When you have completed the survey select one or two responses that you would like to reflect and focus on. In your journal tell more about that choice and come up with one way that you can improve that social connection. You can also log these goals into the action plan at the end of this chapter.

	Not at all like me	A little like me	Sort of like me	A lot like me	Very much like me
I have healthy, connected relationships with my family	1	2	3	4	5
I have people in my life that I look up to	1	2	3	4	5
I have people in my life that enjoy the same activities and we enjoy them together	1	2	3	4	5
I feel accepted by my friends and family	1	2	3	4	5
I feel like a belong to a community	1	2	3	4	5
I have someone to spend the holidays and special occasions together	1	2	3	4	5
I feel disconnected from others	1	2	3	4	5
I feel lonely and isolated from others	1	2	3	4	5
I am involved in community service, faith-based volunteering, or some other act of service that helps me stay connected	1	2	3	4	5
I have a relationship with a higher power and share it with others	1	2	3	4	5

"We don't accomplish anything in this world alone...and whatever happens is the result of the whole tapestry of one's life and all the weavings of individual threads from one to another that creates something."

–Sandra Day O'Connor

Activity 2: Who Are Your Social Connections?

Goal: To look at your social connections and the diversity among them

Let's take a look at your social connections and the diversity of those connections. Answer the questions based on the majority representation of a culture for the question. Think about the following racial/ethnic demographics:

Black Culture

White Culture

Latin/Hispanic Culture

Asian/Pacific Island Culture

Indigenous Culture

all other Cultures

1. Who do you work with or go to school with (think about the people you choose at school at work – (i.e. at lunch who do you eat with; in class who will you choose to sit next to)?

2. Who lives in your neighborhood?

3. Who is part of your friend circle?

4. Who were the last 3 people that came to visit your home?

5. What shows do you watch on TV?

6. Look at the layout of your pipe cleaners.

7. What do you notice about the diversity of your groups?

8. How do you think that impacts your social connections?

This information is important when identifying the connections in your life as well as thinking about what connections you can add to your life.

collectively

Activity 3: Social Connections Bingo

Goal: Encourage social connection through common activities

Time to play Bingo! Share this activity with family and friends and invite them to play with you. Share your progress along the way! The more connected you are, the healthier you will be!

To get BINGO mark the box of the activity you did (use stickers, color it in, cross it out – whatever you would like). Once you have 5 boxes marked in a row (horizontal, vertical, diagonal) you have BINGO! Congratulations!

Pick one or two of the activities and reflect on them.

- Were you uncomfortable with it?
- How did it go?
- How did you feel when you completed the activity?
- How can you incorporate that activity into your daily life?

B	I	N	G	O
Take a walk and say hello to someone new	Deep breathe and picture someone you are grateful for	Try a new hobby & tell someone about it	Wave to your neighbor	Try learning a new skill and sharing it with someone
Create a daily affirmation for yourself	Volunteer	Smile at a stranger	Have a picnic with family/friends	Have a family/friend game night
Talk to someone younger than you and ask them about a current event that is important to them	List 2 people you would like to know better and reach out	FREE SQUARE	Connect with an older adult in your life	Cook a new recipe with others (in-person or virtually)
Write a letter to a family member or friend	Have a meal with a friend	Call an old friend	List 4 people you are thankful for and tell them	Find one person that has the same hobby as you
Experience nature: go for a hike, bike ride, camping, etc	Give a compliment	Try a new food and tell someone about it	Invite someone to have dessert with (in person or virtual)	Send an encouraging text message

Activity 4: Strengthen Your Connections

Goal: Identify how you are supported and how you support your relationships

Social connections are the relationships we have with the people around us. The relationships we have at school, work, socially, and at home impact our physical and mental health.

List 3 people who support you and one type of support you get from each of them.
Example: Friend – listens to me when I am anxious

_____

_____

_____

Write how you support your list of people.
Example: Friend – participate in carpool with the kids

_____

_____

_____

_____

_____

_____

What is one thing you can do this week to connect with them?
Example: Sister – I can call her and have a "catch-up" chat

_____

_____

_____

_____

_____

_____

_____

Activity 5: Making Meaningful Connections

Goal: Find ways to strengthen your connections or make new ones

It's not easy to break the cycle of isolation and loneliness. Challenges such as worry, fear, or health can be a barrier to reaching out to others. The more you practice connection, the easier it gets; and it will make you feel better.

How can you discover ways to strengthen your current connections or make new connections? Think about your strengths, talents, or interests when looking at volunteer opportunities.

Watch the video "Building Social Connections" https://www.youtube.com/watch?v=8az-gfljEbg

Using your computer or smart phone, look for activities or volunteer opportunities that will help with making connections. What did you find?

_____

_____

Reflect/Discussion:

- What were some of the opportunities you found that seemed interesting to you?

- What made them interesting?

- How could this improve your social connection?

_____

_____

_____

_____

_____

_____

_____

_____

Activity 6: Making a Connection Capsule

Goal: To create something special for someone meaningful in your life

A connection capsule is similar to a time capsule with one exception, a time capsule collects the items of a time period whereas a connection capsule collects items of a meaningful relationship.

The connection capsule is filled with special items that you will give to someone meaningful in your life. This may be a great opportunity to reconnect with someone from the past or someone you see in your daily life.

It just takes a few steps to create. BE CREATIVE! There is no limit to what you can put in your connection capsule, the object you use to create the capsule, or how you decorate it. It can be simple or elaborate… IT IS YOUR CHOICE!

1. Select your container

2. Decide what to include. Items such as (but you are not limited to these):

    -   Pictures

    -   Mementos from outings you've shared

    -   A list of things you both have in common

    -   Written memories

    -   Written hopes, thoughts, note of appreciation

    -   Anything you feel will connect you with the recipient

3. Put it all together and deliver it: arrange all the items in your container. You can add a note for each item or a note that tells the recipient what the container is all about.

Sample Note

> *Hi there.*
>
> *I created this "connection capsule" just for you. It's filled with items that represent our journey together. In it you'll find items that have special meaning to our (friendship, relationship). Enjoy looking through the capsule and know that you are never far from my mind and heart.*
>
> *(Love) (All the best),*

Activity 7: The Chain

Goal: Link players through common bonds

To start the game, the first player makes a statement (anything they choose to share). Another player that can relate to that statement becomes the next link in the chain. For example: "I love walking my dog", the next player has to agree that they like walking their dog, and then add on what they want to share.

The game is usually played in the same room and people jump in to add to the chain by linking arms with the person they are "connecting to". It can also be done virtually by using the raise hand feature.

Activity 8: Common Bonds

Goal: Identify commonalities within groups

To play this game, send people in groups (or breakout rooms) for 3-5 minutes. Each team must find three things that everyone in the group has in common. Then process as a large group to let people share their common bonds. Play again by mixing up the groups.

collectively

Activity 9: Getting to Know You; Getting to Know All About You

Goal: Recognize how getting to know someone without judgment can improve social connection

Instructions: without speaking, look at your partner and answer the questions below. Once you have completed the judgment column, then have a conversation to learn the reality. Take turns learning about each other.

QUESTION	JUDGMENT	REALITY
Where was this person born?		
How would they define their ancestry/ethnicity		
What does this person do to relax?		
What is this person's favorite hobby?		
What is their favorite junk food?		
What do they like to watch on television?		
As a child, how would this person have answered this question: "When I grow up, I want to be..."		

What was your takeaway from this activity?

_____

_____

Activity 10: Make Eye Contact

Goal: Recognize how making eye contact builds connection

As a group activity invite participants to get into pairs. Start the clock and instruct them to make eye contact for the next 30 seconds.

As an individual activity: The next conversation with someone you know, be intentional about making eye contact (not in a gazing way) but truly looking in their eyes. Notice if you feel more connected.

Reflection (group or individual)

Did you feel any discomfort making eye contact? Why?

_____

_____

_____

Was there a moment during those 30 seconds that you stopped feeling discomfort? If so, when? If not, why did you continue making eye contact?

_____

_____

_____

Did you feel more connected with that person?

_____

_____

_____

Discuss as a large group

Activity 11: Tell Me More

Goal: Understand that active listening builds connection

Often our communication involves thinking about what we are going to say next in the conversation rather than actively listening to what the other person is saying or what they need. Be intentional about stopping, slowing down, being present and actively listening to the other person.

This is a great activity for making connections through listening: Ask someone to think about a time in their life that they were truly happy, a story that makes them laugh, or a special event that was positive.

One person will be the storyteller and the other will be the listener. Take turns.

Listener: These are some prompts that can help the storyteller get started. Select one and ask the storyteller.

- Where were you?
- What was going on?
- What were you doing?
- Who else was there?
- What made it such a memorable experience?
- How did it make you feel then?
- How does it make you feel now looking back?
- Try to picture being there again

Be an active listener by helping them savor every aspect of the story as they recount it by asking questions that will amplify the positive memories for them.

Storyteller: As you prepare to share your experience, take a moment to describe it in detail;

- Where were you?
- What was going on?
- What were you doing?
- Who else was there?
- What made it such a memorable experience?
- How did it make you feel then?
- How does it make you feel now looking back?
- Try to picture being there again

Activity 12: Smiling's My Favorite

Goal: Know that smiling creates connection

A smile costs nothing, but it can add at least seven years to your life.

Researchers have found that the secret to a longer life lies in cracking a smile. A smile is an outward sign of perceived self-confidence and internal satisfaction. It seems to have a favorable influence upon others and makes one likeable and more approachable. Go to the link below to learn more:

https://www.dailymail.co.uk/health/article-1265548/Smiling-add-years-life.html

Make a conscious effort to smile at 5 people today and notice the responses you receive.

Reflect:

How did you feel smiling at them?

_____

_____

How did they react?

_____

_____

Activity 13: Flip the Script

Goal: Recognize how we can take responsibility to connect to others

The best way to make social connections is to be the change you want to see. We often get in our own heads and feel that we are being left out, people don't reach out to us, and we are all alone or lonely. Rather than sitting around and waiting to be invited, flip the script. Be the person that reaches out to others and the one that includes others. Perhaps you want to be included by one person in particular and they don't reach out, which makes you sad. The best thing you can do is to make a decision to intentionally connect with others.

Identify a person that you would like to spend time with:

_____

How will you reach out to them:

_____

_____

If that doesn't work, who is another person that you would like to spend time with?

_____

_____

How will you reach out to them?

_____

_____

This can feel very vulnerable and scary so before you reach out plan what you want to say and write it down.

_____

_____

Activity 14: Write a Letter

Goal: Recognize how handwritten notes foster social connection

A handwritten note goes a long way- especially since it is a dying art. Take a minute to write a note of gratitude to someone you want to connect with. The simple act of writing the note (rather than texting) and delivering the note will create more of a connection. Use a note card or stationery that you really like. Here's an example of a letter:

Dear _____,

I just wanted to take a moment to write you a note/letter of thanks and appreciation. Thank you for _____. It really made me feel _____

_____. Our friendship/relationship

is so important to me because _____. I just wanted to tell

you how much I value you in my life.

Activity 15: Connections Calendar

Goal: Recognize how daily connections can improve mental health

WEEK 1	WEEK 2	WEEK 3	WEEK 4
Call a friend to catch up and be an active listener	Make plans to meet a friend for a meal	Send an encouraging message to someone who needs boost	Thank someone and tell them how they made a difference
Check in with someone who you have not heard from in a long time	If you see a neighbor say "hello" and have a chat	Set an intention to respond kindly today (even to yourself)	Support a local business with a positive online review or message
Send a message to let someone know you are thinking of them	Tell 3 people that you are thankful for them and tell them why	Show an interest by asking questions when talking to others	Appreciate the good qualities of someone in your life
Give a positive comment to 2 people	Make plans to meet with family/friends and do a fun activity	Get back in touch with someone you have not connected with in a while	Write a thank you note to someone meaningful in your life
Compliment someone on something OTHER than physical appearance	During a conversation today focus on being kind, not right	Share what you are feeling with someone you really trust	Smile at someone who looks like they need a smile
Ask a friend how they have been feeling recently	Share something that you find helpful or amusing with one other person	Look for good in someone that is making you feel frustrated (including yourself)	Tell a loved one about the strength you see in them
Do an act of kindness to make life easier for someone	Schedule uninterrupted time with someone meaningful in your life	Tell a person that is meaningful to you why they are special to you	Be gentle and listen without judgment

Activity 16: What Does Friendship Mean to Us?

Goal: Build on why friendship is important

Answer the following questions:

What qualities do I admire in a friend?

_____

_____

_____

Why are these qualities important to me?

_____

_____

_____

What do I like to do with my friends?

_____

_____

What feelings do I have when I am with my friends?

_____

_____

What makes a good friend?

_____

_____

What makes me a good friend?

_____

_____

_____

collectively

Activity 17: Speed Connecting

Goal: Learn that quick conversations create connections

Participants will have three minutes to find a partner and ask them three questions each. At the end of three minutes, the facilitator will say switch partners and the pair will need to find other people to connect with. In the second grouping, the pair will have three minutes to ask three questions. At the end of the three minutes, the facilitator will instruct the pair to find two different partners and the final pairing will have three minutes to ask three questions of each other. At the end of the activity, process if they felt connected to each partner.

Activity 18: Breaking Bread

Goal: Identify ways to make connections that match our culture

Many people connect over food – we break bread as a society. Take a moment to think about how your culture makes connections over food.

_____

_____

If you were going to prepare a meal to connect over, what food would be included?

_____

_____

Who would you want to share this meal with? Now think about making that connection. A simple request could be as simple as, "I am really craving _____, want to join me for our favorite food?"

_____

_____

_____

Activity 19: Take Up Your Favorite Hobby

Goal: Build connections through a preferred activity with like-minded people

When we participate in a favorite hobby, it brings us joy. Further, if our hobby is something that can be done around others, we will be in the vicinity of like-minded people. Say for example you like art. If you were to take an art class, there is a likelihood that you would be in a class with others that also like art. This would allow you the opportunity to chat about art before, during, and after class. When you have something in common with someone, the conversation will flow easier, and you will feel more connected.

Take a moment to think about three favorite hobbies:

_____

_____

_____

Which of these hobbies has the potential for building connections with others:

_____

_____

_____

Identify how you can begin to practice this hobby around others:

_____

_____

_____

Activity 20: Transformational Action Plan

Goal: Using the activities, select two to improve your social connections

What change(s) are you going to make to improve your social connections?

AREA FOR GROWTH	
STRENGTHS RESOURCES	
ACTION STEPS	
WHO SUPPORTS GROWTH	
TIME FRAME	

collectively

Chapter 2 ~ Social Support

What if I tell you that I have the recipe for a magic potion that when used will help you live longer, have less stress in your life, have better cardiovascular health, and have increased immunity. What if I also say that using this potion will decrease your risk of mental health and substance use conditions, you will have decreased risk of Alzheimer's and you will even think faster! In fact, research demonstrates that using this potion improves overall psychological and physical well being in both adults and children. So, what's this amazing potion you ask? The secret ingredient is simply… social support.

Social support is often identified as a key component of solid relationships and strong mental health, but what exactly is social support? Social support is defined as supportive relationships and access to social networks inclusive of structural or functional support comprised of the following functions: emotional, tangible, informational, and companionship support. Social support can be either actual or perceived and includes the support dynamics of reciprocity, mutuality, and equality.

Essentially, social support means having a network of family, faith, and friends that you can turn to in times of need. This need for social support is universal!

Life has certainly changed over the past few years! Have you ever wondered why some people are able to weather the storm while others struggle to cope with the changes? The research of Suniya Luthar, professor emerita at Columbia University, identified that "the most resilient children tended to have strong relationships with caregivers they trust who make them feel listened to and loved." It's social support that helps adults and children deal with stress and give them the strength to move forward, and even thrive!

There are many ways to obtain social support and the research shows that participation in social groups has influence on behaviors including whether people eat a healthy diet, exercise, smoke, drink, or use illegal substances. Think about a time in your life when you were trying to start a healthy habit or give up a bad one; did social support impact your outcome?

An amazing aspect of social support is that it is incredibly equalizing. You don't have to be wealthy to have support. Support does not pay attention to race, ethnicity, age, or gender. Support can be low cost/ no cost and is accessible to most. Like most important aspects in our lives, when we prioritize a need, we can make great strides.

COVID has really created a challenge for many in the space of social support. The past few years have impacted the mental wellbeing of most everyone. For many, the workplace environment was a source of social support and when people began working from home, access to that support was changed. For some they had to travel to see their families and that became a barrier. When you think of our youth, schools were shut down for a spell, then some children went back in person others continued virtually.

Even wearing a mask is isolating and has an impact on connection- it's difficult to see if someone is smiling. When we are armed with the knowledge of the benefits of social support, it makes it easier to prioritize it in our lives. Remember, the grass is always greener where you water it.

How do you know when you need to enhance your social support systems and what can you do about it? When it comes to support, if you find yourself feeling lonely, isolated, or lacking in support systems, it's important to assess your relationships.

The best way to build support is to begin with the relationships you already have. Identify what is working in that relationship and assess how you can expand it. One of the biggest barriers to having a meaningful support system is our ability to ask for help. It's hard to be vulnerable, and often our fear gets in the way. According to Brene Brown, "vulnerability is anything but weak, in fact, it takes true strength and courage to allow yourself to be vulnerable". In her Ted Talk, The Power of Vulnerability she inspires people to practice vulnerability because "vulnerability is the birthplace of connection and the path to feeling worthy and true belonging". This speaks to not only the quantity of your support but also the quality of your support.

Additionally, finding happiness in activities that brings you joy provides an amazing opportunity for connection and support. When you are passionate about something, and you enjoy that activity, it increases endorphins in your body which gives you energy. Further, when doing an activity that you truly enjoy, you are likely to meet others also enjoying the same activity. Therein lies the opportunity for expanding your support system!

Here are some activities you may use to assess, identify, build, and cultivate your support systems.

Activity 1: Friends, Family, and Faith

Goal: Understand that social supports come in many forms

Write down or make a mental note of a time in your own personal life when you were struggling. This should be a time when you needed support from others.

_____

_____

Now, answer the following questions while you are thinking about your challenge:

How did you get through this challenge?

_____

_____

What supports were the most critical to you?

_____

_____

Consider the following questions: Mark an **x** next to each one that applies to you

- ☐ Were you able to get through your challenge with the help of your family?
- ☐ Were you able to get through your challenge with the help of your friends?
- ☐ Were you able to get through your challenge with the help of your faith?
- ☐ Were you able to get through your challenge with the help of assistance of a paid professional with an advanced degree?

Look at all the questions marked with an x.

Did you need the help of a paid professional or did you rely more on your family, faith, and friends for support?

_____

_____

The majority of people recognize that they turn more to their family, faith, and friends for support then to a paid professional with an advanced degree. You'll learn more about building your supports in the coming chapters.

Activity 2: Social Support Survey

Goal: Identify your social supports

Please complete the following assessment to recognize the social supports in your life.

	None of the time	A little of the time	Some of the time	Most of the time	All of the time
I feel connected to my network of social supports	1	2	3	4	5
I have friends that are there for me	1	2	3	4	5
My family supports me	1	2	3	4	5
I have a people in my life that I can count on	1	2	3	4	5
There is someone in my life, other than family, that I can count on	1	2	3	4	5
I have someone I can talk to when I need support	1	2	3	4	5
If I were not feeling well, I feel that I have someone will take care of me	1	2	3	4	5
There is someone in my life that shows me love and affection	1	2	3	4	5
I feel supported by a faith community	1	2	3	4	5
I have someone in my life that gives me good advice	1	2	3	4	5

This survey was created by the Rand Corporation- see resources section for a link.

collectively

What did you learn from this assessment?

_____

_____

_____

_____

What areas of support will you focus on increasing in your life?

_____

_____

_____

"A person in need of support, looks a lot more like a person in need of mental health treatment, than a person with support."

–Unknown

Activity 3: Social Support Questions

Goal: Identify social supports

Below are some questions that you can answer around support:

Who do I trust? Tell more about them.

_____

Do I have neighbors, friends, or family members who are aware of my situation and can help me? Tell more about them.

_____

Are there any activities in my community that interest me? List those activities.

_____

What are my spiritual or religious activities? What kind are they and how often do I go?

_____

Who is my emergency contact? Tell more about them.

_____

If my car breaks down, whom will I call? Tell more about them.

_____

Who helps me now? Who has helped me in the past? Tell more about those people.

_____

Who helps my family? Tell more about them.

_____

Who do I call when I need to vent or are sad about something? Tell more about them.

_____

Who do I have fun with? Tell more about them.

_____

Who are the last five people I called or texted? Tell more about them.

_____

Activity 4: Ecogram

Goal: Identify social supports in different domains (for example: family you live with, extended family, friends, neighborhood, school/work, clubs/groups, faith community, community)

Let's use an Ecogram to identify Support Systems. Place your name in the center circle and identify potential supports in each domain in the outside circles. Potential domains include: Educational, Residential, Neighborhood/Community, Faith-Based Organization, Vocational...

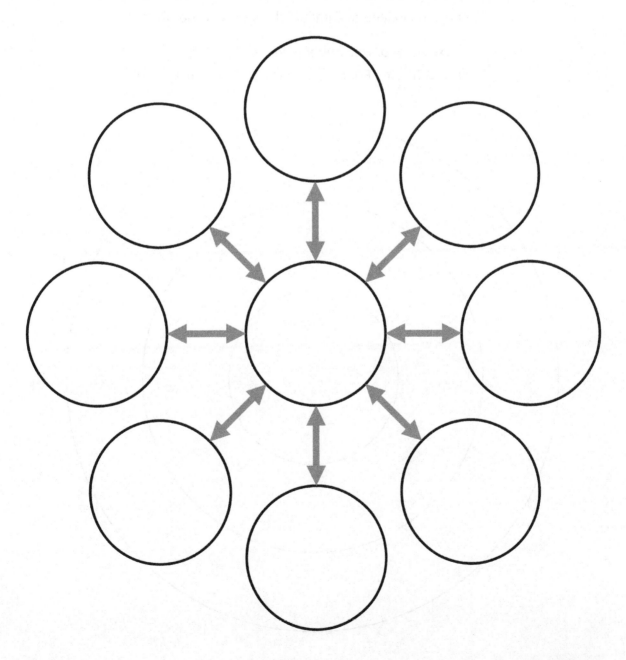

Activity 5: Circle of Support

Goal: Identify who you can ask for help

When facing any challenge it can be helpful to know whom you can count on. Different people may be helpful in different situations. Use the circles below to write down the names of people who you know you can ask for support or help.

Examples of who might fit in the Outer Circle:
Professionals, Helpful Neighbors, Community Members, Acquaintances, Colleagues

Examples of who might fit in the Middle Circle:
Friends and Extended Family, Fellow Church Members

Examples of who might fit in the Inner Circle:
Close and Trusted Friends, Supportive Family Members

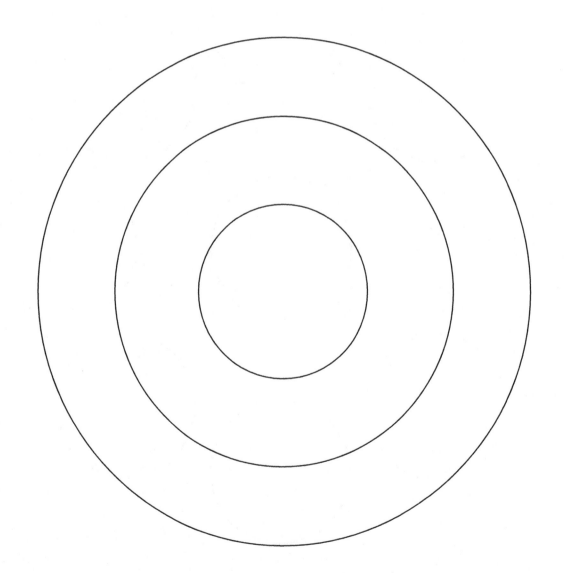

Activity 6: Developing Social Supports

Goal: Create a plan to have positive peer relationships in your community

You want to create **positive peer relationships** in your community. Answer the following questions with the goal in mind.

What are some strengths needed in order to create positive relationships in my community (what do I like to do?):

_____

Brainstorm at least 10 community options that would meet this need while building on strengths. Circle one option that interests me the most.

1. _____

2. _____

3. _____

4. _____

5. _____

6. _____

7. _____

8. _____

9. _____

10. _____

Who could help me get involved in the option I circled?

_____

Develop an action plan for getting started.

STEP	PERSON	DATE

Activity 7: Find My 5

Goal: Identify 5 people you can ask for support

Access to support is a game changer! When we have people to share ideas with, ask for support when we need it, or easily connect with to say thanks, we are happier and healthier.

This activity is designed to help you create your virtual support system. Pre-identifying your support people and creating your support chat is the most important piece to successfully accessing support.

PLEASE TAKE SOME TIME TO ANSWER THE FOLLOWING QUESTIONS TO IDENTIFY WHO YOUR **MY 5** GROUP WOULD BE:

When something goes well for you, who do you want to tell?

When you get a text or call from this person you always answer.

Who do you celebrate your holidays with?

Who do you ask for help with something big (like a move)?

Who have you helped in the past?

Who do you share your struggles with?

Once you have identified your group, reach out to them individually and ask if they are comfortable being on a group text with the others you have identified as your 5. You may want to set up some rules about frequency of chatting or what to chat about or not chat about as some people do not like very active group texts.

Once everyone has agreed, create a chat group and you can start it with this introduction message:

WELCOME TO MY 5!

Thank you for agreeing to be a part of my 5. I may reach out from time to time when I need support. Please take a moment to respond when I reach out-asking for help is hard but we all need to do it! I hope that if you need help you will also reach out through this chat. Thanks for going on this journey with me.

Activity 8: Lean On Me Song

Goal: After listening to this song, identify how this song can help provide and identify social supports

Listen to the song "Lean on Me" by Bill Withers. Copyright 1972 ~Mattie Music Group. Please look at some of the lines listed below and answer the questions related to Social Support.

Please swallow your pride
If I have things you need to borrow
For no one can fill those of your needs
That you won't let show

How do these lyrics encourage you to reach out to your social supports?

_____

_____

_____

If there is a load you have to bear
That you can't carry
I'm right up the road
I'll share your load

How do these lyrics encourage you to reach out to your social supports?

_____

_____

_____

You just call on my brother, when you need a hand
We all need somebody to lean on
I just might have a problem that you'll understand
We all need somebody to lean on

What aspect of social support do these words talk about?

_____

_____

_____

Activity 9: My Social Network

Goal: Reflect on the impact of your social network

Spend a few minutes thinking about your social network.

Who do I spend time with in life?

_____

During the day?

_____

At night?

_____

On the weekends?

_____

During holidays?

_____

Do I connect more in person or online?

_____

How satisfied am I with my current support system?(Scale of 1 {not satisfied}-10 {extremely satisfied})

_____

How well do I feel I know my top three supports?

_____

_____

_____

Who would I like to get to know more?

_____

Reflection

_____

collectively

Activity 10: Ways to Build Support System

Goal: Find Ways to Build Your Support System

1. Identify and join an online or in-person group that aligns with my interest (stick with it for at least three months)

   _____

   _____

2. Get involved in my local community or faith-based organization

   _____

   _____

3. Take an online or in person class

   _____

   _____

4. Invite someone to coffee or for a walk

   _____

   _____

5. What are some other ways I can build my support system?

   _____

   _____

Activity 11: Know My Support System

Goal: Identify how much you know about the people in your life

Building support systems starts with learning something about the people in your life.

1. Focus on one domain in my life (work, school, family, friends)…list the names of all of the people in that circle

    Domain: _____

2. Think about what I know about each of them. Make a list for each person.

3. Notice where my list is shortest and take steps to learn more about those individuals.

PERSON	WHAT I KNOW

"How wonderful it is that nobody needs to wait a single moment before starting to improve the world."

–Anne Frank

Activity 12: Flip the Script

Goal: Identify ways to be supportive of others

Be the change we want to see in our support systems- we are often upset when we feel that others are not "there for us". Rather than focusing on what others are not doing for us, why not use our energy to be supportive of others. When we reach out and support others, the theory of reciprocity states that they will naturally then be there for us. Here are some ways to connect:

- Offer to help

- Send a thank you note

- Make an introduction

- Ask for help

- Comment on someone's social media post

- Volunteer

- Celebrate someone

- Be available for one on one time

- Share something about yourself (be vulnerable)

- Do something that they want to do together

- Send an email or text checking in on someone that may be going through a difficult time

- Schedule time to connect each day- actually put it on your calendar

- Set a reminder- think about intentionally connecting with 3 people each day

- When you cook a meal, make extra and share with a friend or neighbor

- If someone is not feeling well, ask how you can support them- swing by and leave something on their doorstep

- We don't have to solve problems for people, just listening helps- make the time to call or see someone with the only purpose of listening

5 ways that I have supported people in the past 60 days are:

1. _____

2. _____

3. _____

4. _____

5. _____

3 people in my life that are struggling:

1. _____

2. _____

3. _____

What are potential ways that I could support them?

_____

_____

_____

Here are two ways that I will connect with and support the people in my support system

1. _____

2. _____

Activity 13: Personal Culture Assessment

Goal: Assess how your culture plays a part in the support that you have in your life

Culture plays an important role in how we live our life and make decisions. Take a moment to complete the cultural assessment below to assess how your culture plays a part in the support that you have in your life.

In order to promote cultural self-awareness, answer the following questions as honestly as you can. There are NO right or wrong answers. You do not need to share your assessment with others.

Where and when were you born?

_____

Where did you grow up?

_____

Where did your parents and grandparents grow up?

_____

What is your earliest memory as a family?

_____

What types of important issues do you discuss with your family?

_____

When major decisions are made in your family, who participates?

_____

As a family, what events did you celebrate?

_____

As an adult, what events or holidays do you currently celebrate?

_____

What languages do you speak?

_____

c⚙llectively

How do you greet people you don't know?

___

What is a comfortable physical talking distance between you and a colleague?

___

If you smile at someone, what does that mean?

___

Do you consider time linear and finite or more elastic and relative?

___

Do you discuss your thoughts, feelings, and problems with people outside your family? If so, to whom? In what situations?

___

Do you prefer getting information in words or with a diagram? One step at a time or the whole process at once?

___

Do you believe that individuals control their own destiny or that everything happens for a reason?

___

What racial/ethnic/socio-economic groups/religious/gender groups do you identify with?

___

What is your earliest memory of belonging to a group (other than your family)?

___

What is your earliest memory of being excluded from a group?

___

What is your earliest memory of excluding someone from a group?

___

Activity 14: Reflection of Culture and the Path Forward

Goal: Identify the impact of culture on your social supports

Based on the results from activity 13, what are your reflections?

What does my family support look like?

_____

_____

How does my communication style impact connection with others?

_____

_____

What can I do to expand my connection with groups based on my culture?

_____

_____

How does my culture impact my social supports?

_____

_____

Activity 15: Identifying Your Core Values

Goal: Identify how your core values can help create your social supports

When we are living our values we have better mental health. Have you taken time to identify what your values are?

Take a moment to complete this activity to identify your core values. Once you have clarified your values, then you can look to create support in those areas.

How are you showing up in your personal relationships? For yourself? At work/school?

How you show up in the world is determined by your core values.

It doesn't take years of self-reflection to uncover your core values. This simple exercise can help you determine them so you can start aligning your personal goals with them.

1. Determine Your Core Values

From the list below, circle every core value that resonates with you. If you think of a value you possess that is not on the list, write it down.

Abundance	Cheerfulness	Enthusiasm	Independence
Acceptance	Cleverness	Ethics	Individuality
Accountability	Collaboration	Excellence	Innovation
Achievement	Community	Expressiveness	Inspiration
Adventure	Commitment	Fairness	Intelligence
Advocacy	Compassion	Family	Intuition
Ambition	Consistency	Flexibility	Joy
Appreciation	Contribution	Friendships	Kindness
Attractiveness	Cooperation	Freedom	Knowledge
Autonomy	Creativity	Fun	Leadership
Balance	Credibility	Generosity	Learning
Being the Best	Curiosity	Grace	Love
Benevolence	Daring	Growth	Loyalty
Boldness	Decisiveness	Happiness	Making a Difference
Brilliance	Dedication	Health	Mindfulness
Calmness	Dependability	Honesty	Motivation
Caring	Diversity	Humility	Optimism
Challenge	Empathy	Humor	Open-Mindedness
Charity	Encouragement	Inclusiveness	Originality

Passion	Punctuality	Self-Control	Understanding
Performance	Quality	Selflessness	Uniqueness
Personal Development	Recognition	Service	Usefulness
Peace	Relationships	Simplicity	Versatility
Perfection	Reliability	Spirituality	Vision
Playfulness	Resilience	Stability	Warmth
Popularity	Resourcefulness	Success	Wealth
Power	Responsibility	Teamwork	Well-Being
Preparedness	Responsiveness	Thankfulness	Wisdom
Proactivity	Risk Taking	Thoughtfulness	Zeal
Proactive	Safety	Traditionalism	
Professionalism	Security	Trustworthiness	

---

2. Group All Similar Values Together from the List of Values You Just Created

Group them in a way that makes sense to you, personally. Create a maximum of five groupings. If you have more than five groupings, drop the least important grouping(s).

See the example below.

ABUNDANCE	ACCEPTANCE	APPRECIATION	BALANCE	CHEERFULNESS
Growth	Compassion	Encouragement	Health	Fun
Wealth	Inclusiveness	Thankfulness	Personal Development	Happiness
Security	Intuition	Thoughtfulness	Spirituality	Humor
Freedom	Kindness	Mindfulness	Well-being	Inspiration
Independence	Love			Joy
Flexibility	Making a Difference			Optimism
Peace	Open-Mindedness			Playfulness
	Trustworthiness			
	Relationships			

3. Choose One Word Within Each Group that Represents the Label for the Entire Group

Again, do not overthink your labels – there are no right or wrong answers. You are defining the answer that is right for you. See the example below – the label chosen for the grouping is bolded.

ABUNDANCE	ACCEPTANCE	APPRECIATION	BALANCE	CHEERFULNESS
Growth	Compassion	Encouragement	Health	Fun
Wealth	Inclusiveness	Thankfulness	Personal Development	**Happiness**
Security	Intuition	Thoughtfulness	Spirituality	Humor
Freedom	Kindness	**Mindfulness**	**Well-being**	Inspiration
Independence	Love			Joy
Flexibility	**Making a Difference**			Optimism
Peace	Open-Mindedness			Playfulness
	Trustworthiness			
	Relationships			

4. Add a Verb to Each Value Label

Add a verb to each value so you can see what it looks like as an actionable core value.

For example:

Live in freedom.

Seek opportunities for making a difference.

Act with mindfulness.

Promote well-being.

Multiply happiness.

This will guide you in the actions you need to take to feel like you are truly living on purpose.

5. Finally, Post Your Core Values Where You See Them when Faced with Decisions

Where should you post them? Write your core values in order of priority in your planner, so they are available as an easy reference when you are faced with decisions. Put them on a sticky on the edge of your computer screen. Or make a background with them on it for your cell phone. For example:

1. Live in *freedom.*

2. *Act with mindfulness.*

3. *Promote well-being.*

4. *Multiply happiness.*

5. *Seek opportunities for making a difference.*

Now Live Your Core Values! If we can get to the place where we show up as our genuine selves, and let each other see who we really are, the awe-inspiring ripple effect will change the world.

Source: https://www.taproot.com/live-your-core-values-exercise-to-increase-your-success/

Activity 16: Living My Core Values

Goal: Make a Plan to Live Your Core Values

Now that you know your values, identify what you value in a friendship.

_____

_____

_____

How will you use this information to intentionally create support?

_____

_____

_____

How will you work to incorporate your core values into your daily life?

_____

_____

_____

How will you overcome challenges that may impact living your core values?

_____

_____

_____

collectively

Activity 17: Categories of Support

Goal: Identify different people that can be social supports

We can't rely on one person to meet all of our needs. Think about the kinds of relationships you want in your life and who could potentially meet that need. Who in your life meets these categories? Here are some typical categories, write the name of the person in your life that falls into that category for you:

Fun: _____

The Sage (wise friend you seek advice from): _____

Cheerleader: _____

Someone to talk to: _____

Someone to rely on: _____

Someone to just hang with: _____

Someone to challenge you: _____

Planner/organizer: _____

Did you identify a person for every category?

_____

If not, how can you find a person to meet that need?

_____

Activity 18: Proximity Speaks Volumes

Goal: Identify social supports that are close to you

The concept of proximity comes into play when we are talking about support systems. The research around proximity is that when you see someone on a regular basis you form a close connection. Whether we are talking about a neighbor, a co-worker whose office is close to yours or a peer whose desk is near yours in class. When people are proximate, they can be a support to one another.

Five people that are proximate to me are (these may not be your closest/best friends, just think about the people that you converse with in your daily life):

1. _____

2. _____

3. _____

4. _____

5. _____

What do I like about each of these people and how can I nurture that relationship:

1. _____

2. _____

3. _____

4. _____

5. _____

Activity 19: Support Superpowers

Goal: Identify what makes me a good friend

We all have strengths! Have you ever taken the time to identify the aspects of you that makes you a good friend? How are you supporting others? Review the list of friendship qualities and identify what makes a good friend.

1. They are dependable
2. They are supportive
3. They accept you as you are
4. They actively listen
5. They are emotionally available
6. They have similar interests
7. They show up during tough times
8. They are reciprocal
9. They have your best interests in mind
10. They don't just reach out when they need something
11. They are loyal and help you out no matter what
12. They understand "no"
13. They respect your differences
14. They honor boundaries
15. They make you feel safe
16. They make you feel like you can be your real self around them
17. They connect easily with you
18. They are confident in their own identity
19. They are securely attached
20. They celebrate you
21. They are forgiving
22. They express love to you in whatever way they can
23. The conversation goes beyond "small talk" and catching up
24. They hold you accountable if you are self-sabotaging
25. They encourage you rather than disparage you for trying new things
26. They are kind
27. They are honest
28. They are adventurous
29. They are playful
30. They are protective
31. They have clairvoyance
32. They are optimistic but practical
33. They are respectful
34. They are fiercely huggable
35. The sit in silence without awkwardness
36. They are openhearted
37. They are genuinely happy for each other when good things happen
38. They are genuinely excited to see you
39. You feel comfortable enough to ask them for a favor
40. They gently push you out of your comfort zone

What qualities on this list do I strive to incorporate into my life?

_____

Think of the friendships I currently have in my life; what qualities would describe them?

_____

Activity 20: Transformational Action Plan

Goal: Using the activities, select two to improve your social supports

What change(s) are you going to make to improve your social supports?

AREA FOR GROWTH	
STRENGTHS RESOURCES	
ACTION STEPS	
WHO SUPPORTS GROWTH	
TIME FRAME	

Chapter 3 ~ Social Capital

Do you know that in the last twenty years people went from having three close connections to having two close connections? That's a problem because when we have strong social connections in our lives, we live longer than isolated people.

As a researcher of social connectedness, I am often asked, "How can I create better connections in my life?" Seems like a straightforward question, but my typical response is, tell me more about what kind of connections you are looking to create? Feeling connected to another person is very different than feeling connected to your community. Honestly, we need both and one is not more important than the other.

Research demonstrates that we are happier when we have 3-5 strong ties (deep connections). Additionally, we have the capacity to have up to 150 weak ties (friends, co-workers, classmates, or social media connections). It's the combination of strong ties and weak ties that creates a happy, healthy human being.

Sometimes social connections are about people, and sometimes they are about networks and communities. When we are talking about individual connections, we are looking for a support system to help us in times of need. When we're talking about community connections, we're looking for a sense of belonging. According to Healthy Places by Design, "people living in socially connected communities are more likely to thrive because they feel safe, welcome, and trust each other."

Many people struggle with having those 3-5 strong connections in their life, thus, when they need support, they end up in crisis and leaning on government systems. One way to build those 3-5 strong connections is to engage in developing community social capital.

What's Social Capital?

Social Capital is a structure of networks and collective resources within a community that individuals within that community can draw upon and that will benefit them.

Have you ever been involved in a group, sports team or with co-workers and had a need? Just by virtue of having access to others, you were able to ask for advice, seek support, or maybe even benefit from a connection- that's social capital. If you reflect on that situation, did having a relationship with that person help you solve your problem? Research demonstrates that just by thinking you have someone to turn to (perceived support), you have better mental health.

In order to understand social capital, we need to recognize some of its components including:

- Networks- building connections across people and places
- Norms- groups create rules for membership- understanding these "rules" ensures belonging

- Trust (feeling safe)- safety is an important component of any connected group and feeling that you can trust others to follow through builds a sense of community

- Social Support- being there for each other in times of need is central to social capital

- Connections- both connections within the group as well as the willingness to connect others to have their needs met

- Reciprocity (support without return)- this concept means that not only will we accept help from others, but that we are willing to give help. Reciprocity is not doing something with the expectation that someone else will do something for you in return

- Common shared activities (community building activities)- social capital often shows up in the actions of the group. Having a shared mission or vision and then working towards it together builds capital

- Institutional linkage- social capital is both about what you know as well as who you know- making connections to leadership to support the growth of others is an important component of social capital

These days, in communities all over the world, people are struggling with their mental health. Some communities have taken matters into their own hands and are using social capital to address community mental health. Remember the African Friendship Bench program where local "grandmothers" were trained in mental health interventions. The intervention involves sitting on community benches and being available for people in need to join them in conversation. That's a perfect example of social capital- they are taking the strengths in the community (the "grandmothers" who have time and experience) and creating an opportunity to support others in need.

Now, ask yourself this question, how do you think that the "grandmother" feels being a part of Friendship Beach? Not only is she helping someone in need, but she is also part of a solution to improve mental health AND she belongs to an important movement in the community. A similar program is available in the United States called Sidewalk Talk and it has been used in communities all over the country. Programs like these utilize something called abundance thinking, which is a mindset that focuses on community assets rather than on deficits. It is the belief that there are enough resources available and more than enough creativity and wisdom to meet our needs. We build social capital when we recognize, celebrate, and reinforce assets inherent in local communities and acknowledge that every resident has assets and the ability to lead their own change.

Building social capital starts with individual contributions. There are so many ways to build social capital, here are just a few:

- Make time to connect with people: when we take the time to learn about people, we create a connection that can support future community growth.

- Follow through and get things done: people want to work with others who are dependable and hardworking.

- Be positive and optimistic: say yes to invitations to participate in community efforts, boards, and organizations.

- Express Gratitude: gratitude strengthens bonds between people, deepens trust, and expands social capital. People want to be around others who see them, appreciate them, and value their contributions.

- Return the favor: reciprocity is an important component of building relationships.

- Invite others to participate: enlist others along the way and help others build relationship networks.

Building relationships, connections, and social capital takes time and energy. When people invest their time and assets to help the greater good, communities become stronger, create tighter bonds among residents, and build supports to sustain change. Having these connections creates better mental health for individuals as well as the community. Together we can change the narrative on mental health.

Here are some activities you may use to assess, identify, build, and cultivate social capital in your life.

Activity 1: Social Capital Quiz

Goal: Identify your social capital

The social connections we have in our lives are a vital part of our health and happiness, but connections come in many different ways. Someone who is a lifelong friend is typically different than a casual acquaintance you meet online or at work event.

Yet according to research, we need both weak ties and strong ties in order to build "social capital," which researchers define as the web of relationships in our life and the tangible and intangible benefits we derive from them.

So, where does your social capital fall? Does it come from the strong bonds of the people closest to you and likely similar to you?

The following quiz will help you answer those questions. Based on a scale developed by Dmitri Williams, a professor at the University of Illinois, Urbana-Champaign, it measures the amount—and the sources—of social capital in your life.

This quiz contains a total of 9 questions that will measure how much social capital you have. Just pay attention to your answers to get a sense of areas you can improve upon to address later in the chapter.

1. I interact with people who make me interested in what people unlike me are thinking.

   ☐ Strongly Disagree

   ☐ Disagree

   ☐ Neither Agree nor Disagree

   ☐ Agree

   ☐ Strongly Agree

2. I am willing to spend time to support general community activities.

   ☐ Strongly Disagree

   ☐ Disagree

   ☐ Neither Agree nor Disagree

   ☐ Agree

   ☐ Strongly Agree

3. Interacting with people gives me new people to talk to.

   ☐ Strongly Disagree

   ☐ Disagree

   ☐ Neither Agree nor Disagree

   ☐ Agree

   ☐ Strongly Agree

4. If I needed an emergency loan of $500, I know people I could turn to.

   ☐ Strongly Disagree

   ☐ Disagree

   ☐ Neither Agree nor Disagree

   ☐ Agree

   ☐ Strongly Agree

5. I interact with people who remind me that everyone in the world is connected.

    ☐ Strongly Disagree

    ☐ Disagree

    ☐ Neither Agree nor Disagree

    ☐ Agree

    ☐ Strongly Agree

6. There are people I interact with who would be good job references for me.

    ☐ Strongly Disagree

    ☐ Disagree

    ☐ Neither Agree nor Disagree

    ☐ Agree

    ☐ Strongly Agree

7. I interact with people who make me feel like part of a larger community.

    ☐ Strongly Disagree

    ☐ Disagree

    ☐ Neither Agree nor Disagree

    ☐ Agree

    ☐ Strongly Agree

8. I interact with people who make me feel connected to the bigger picture.

    ☐ Strongly Disagree

    ☐ Disagree

    ☐ Neither Agree nor Disagree

    ☐ Agree

    ☐ Strongly Agree

9. There are people I interact with who would put their reputation on the line for me.

    ☐ Strongly Disagree

    ☐ Disagree

    ☐ Neither Agree nor Disagree

    ☐ Agree

    ☐ Strongly Agree

Source: https://greatergood.berkeley.edu/quizzes/take_quiz/social_capital

Activity 2: Social Capital Questions

Goal: Learn to identify who is important in your life

In the next three minutes, answer the following questions (without looking up the answers):

The five wealthiest people in the world

1. _____
2. _____
3. _____
4. _____
5. _____

The last five TIME magazine's people of the year

1. _____
2. _____
3. _____
4. _____
5. _____

Five Nobel or Pulitzer Prize Winners

1. _____
2. _____
3. _____
4. _____
5. _____

Last five Best Picture, Best Actor, or Best Actress Academy Award Winners

1. _____
2. _____
3. _____
4. _____
5. _____

collectively

Now, in the next three minutes, answer the following questions:

List five teachers, coaches, or friends that have:

1. _____
2. _____
3. _____
4. _____
5. _____

Aided your journey through life (how)

1. _____
2. _____
3. _____
4. _____
5. _____

Taught you something worthwhile (what)

1. _____
2. _____
3. _____
4. _____
5. _____

Have helped you through a difficult time (how)

1. _____
2. _____
3. _____
4. _____
5. _____

Reflection:

Which was easier and more impactful?

_____

What's the lesson here?

_____

Activity 3: Social Capital Video

Goal: Identify three ways you are already building social capital

Scan one of the QR codes below to watch a video, then answer the reflection questions.

After watching the video can you identify 3 ways you already have built your social capital?

_____

_____

_____

What are some other ways to add to your social capital?

_____

_____

_____

_____

c⊙llectively

"The grass is greener where you water it."

–Neil Barringham

Activity 4: Heroes, Allies, and Companions

Goal: Identify "Heroes," "Allies," and "Worthy Companions"

Divide paper into three parts, titling each section, "Heroes," "Allies," and "Worthy Companions."

Identify and draw artistic representations of people for each box.

Heroes are people that you look up to and admire for their achievements or way of being.

Allies are those who have more power than you that you trust or can enlist to help you move toward your goals.

Worthy Companions are peers who are on a similar journey or could be a good support to you in your journey.

Heroes

Allies

Worthy Companions

Activity 5: 100 Things You Can Do to Build Social Capital

Goal: Build your social capital

You can build social capital without even realizing that is what you are doing. The hundreds of little and big actions you take every day build it!

Take a look at the list below and identify the top three ways you build social capital every day! If you don't see ones on there that you identify with then create your own.

1. Organize a social gathering to welcome a new neighbor
2. Attend town meetings
3. Register to vote and vote
4. Support local merchants
5. Volunteer your special skills to an organization
6. Donate blood
7. Start a community garden
8. Mentor someone of a different ethnic or religious group
9. Surprise a new neighbor by making a favorite dinner–and include the recipe
10. Record your parents' earliest recollections and share them with your children
11. Plan a vacation with friends or family
12. Don't gossip
13. Help fix someone's flat tire
14. Organize or participate in a sports league
15. Join a gardening club
16. Attend home parties when invited
17. Become an organ donor
18. Attend your children's athletic contests, plays and recitals
19. Get to know your children's teachers
20. Join the local Elks, Kiwanis, or Knights of Columbus
21. Get involved with Brownies or Cub/Boy/Girl Scouts
22. Start a monthly tea group
23. Speak at or host a monthly brown bag lunch series at your local library
24. Sing in a choir
25. Get to know the clerks and salespeople at your local stores
26. Attend PTA meetings
27. Audition for community theater or volunteer to usher
28. Give your park a weatherproof chess/checkers board
29. Play cards with friends or neighbors
30. Give to your local food bank

31. Participate in walk-a-thons

32. Employers: encourage volunteer/community groups to hold meetings on your site

33. Volunteer in your child's classroom or chaperone a field trip

34. Join or start a babysitting cooperative

35. Attend school plays

36. Answer surveys when asked

37. Businesses: invite local government officials to speak at your workplace

38. Attend Memorial Day parades and express appreciation for others

39. Form a local outdoor activity group

40. Participate in political campaigns

41. Attend a local budget committee meeting

42. Form a computer group for local senior citizens

43. Help coach Little League or other youth sports – even if you don't have a kid playing

44. Help run the snack bar at the Little League field

45. Form a "tools cooperative" with neighbors and share ladders, snow blowers, etc.

46. Start a lunch gathering or a discussion group with coworkers

47. Offer to rake a neighbor's yard or shovel his/her walk

48. Join a carpool

49. Employers: give employees time (e.g., 3 days per year to work on civic projects)

50. Plan a "Walking Tour" of a local historic area

51. Eat breakfast at a local gathering spot on Saturdays

52. Have family dinners and read to your children

53. Run for public office

54. Stop and make sure the person on the side of the highway is OK

55. Host a block party or a holiday open house

56. Start a fix-it group–friends willing to help each other clean, paint, garden, etc.

57. Offer to serve on a town committee

58. Join the volunteer fire department

59. Go to church...or temple...or go outside with your children–talk to them about spirituality

60. If you grow tomatoes, plant extra for an lonely elder who lives nearby – better yet, ask him/her to teach you and others how to can the extras

61. Ask a single diner to share your table for lunch

62. Stand at a major intersection holding a sign for your favorite candidate

63. Persuade a local restaurant to have a designated "meet people" table

64. Host a potluck supper before your Town Meeting

65. Take dance lessons with a friend

66. Say "thanks" to public servants – police, firefighters, town clerk...

67. Fight to keep essential local services in the downtown area–your post office, police station, school, etc.

68. Join a nonprofit board of directors

69. Gather a group to clean up a local park or cemetery

70. When somebody says "government stinks," suggest they help fix it

71. Turn off the TV and talk with friends or family

72. Hold a neighborhood barbecue

73. Bake cookies for new neighbors or work colleagues

74. Plant tree seedlings along your street with neighbors and rotate care for them

75. Volunteer at the library

76. Form or join a bowling team

77. Return a lost wallet or appointment book

78. Use public transportation and start talking with those you regularly see

79. Ask neighbors for help and reciprocate

80. Go to a local folk or crafts festival

81. Call an old friend

82. Register for a class – then go

83. Accept or extend an invitation

84. Talk to your kids or parents about their day

85. Say hello to strangers

86. Log off and go to the park

87. Ask a new person to join a group for a dinner or an evening

88. Participate in pot luck meals

89. Volunteer to drive someone

90. Say hello when you spot an acquaintance in a store

91. Host a movie night

92. Exercise together or take walks with friends or family

93. Assist with or create your town or neighborhood's newsletter

94. Organize a neighborhood litter pick-up – with lawn games afterwards

95. Collect oral histories from older town residents

96. Join a book club discussion or get the group to discuss local issues

97. Volunteer to deliver Meals-on-Wheels in your neighborhood

98. Start a children's story hour at your local library

99. Be real. Be humble. Acknowledge others' self-worth

100.   Tell friends and family about social capital and why it matters

Write your choices here:

_____

_____

_____

Activity 6: Understanding Reciprocity

Goal: Identify reciprocal relationships

rec·i·proc·i·ty

/ˌresəˈpräsədē/

noun

1. the practice of exchanging things with others for mutual benefit

In 1974, sociologist Phillip Kunz conducted an experiment. He mailed out handwritten Christmas cards with a note and photograph of him and his family to approximately 600 randomly selected people. All of the recipients of the cards were complete strangers. Shortly after mailing the cards, responses began trickling in. Kunz received nearly 200 replies. Why would so many people reply to a complete stranger? This is the rule of reciprocity at work. Since Kunz had done something for them (sent a thoughtful note during the holiday season), many recipients felt obligated to return the favor.

Why is reciprocity important?

Reciprocal behavior: The norm of reciprocity suggests that when people do something helpful for someone else, that person feels compelled to help out in return. This norm developed, evolutionary psychologists suggest, because people who understood that helping others might lead to reciprocal kindness were more likely to survive and reproduce.

Think about the relationships in your life and identify if they are reciprocal. If not, list what you can do to support the goals of others in your life.

_____

_____

_____

_____

_____

Activity 7: Theory of Reciprocity

Goal: Practice reciprocity

People like people who like them.

A study conducted in 1958 brought strangers together in a group to talk about how to improve a class. They all took personality tests, and they received bogus information that three group members were predicted to like them the most based on the test. At the end of the class the researchers told them that they can be divided into groups, and they should report whom they wanted to be grouped with. People chose to pair with people they believed liked them.

We think people like us for so many reasons; research demonstrates the most important quality is that friends made them feel good about themselves. People who excel at making friends have one thing in common, THEY MAKE PEOPLE FEEL LIKE THEY MATTER.

Activity: choose one person today and tell them 2-3 things that you like about them.

Chosen friend: _____

What I like about you:

_____

_____

_____

_____

_____

Activity 8: Risk Relegation Theory

Goal: Being a good friend

Ever heard of the Risk Regulation Theory?

This theory identifies that confidence in a partner's positive regard and caring allows people to risk seeking dependence and connectedness.

In other words, in order to invest in a relationship, we need proof we won't be rejected when doing so. So, if we want people to invest in us, we need to make them feel safe. We show love, we value, and we accept someone so that they can feel safe to take the risk of intimacy with us.

Although we crave connection, we also tend to focus on our needs. When we stop thinking about whether we belong and shift to making others feel like they belong, we'll inevitably belong too.

Activity: Practice how to be a good friend- Think about a special person in your life and how you can celebrate them and be there just for them, without expectations of what they will do for you.

Which friend have you identified? _____

Now, practice asking questions, expressing joy, and being positive. What will you ask them?

_____

_____

_____

_____

_____

_____

Activity 9: Send a Note of Thanks

Goal: Building reciprocity by saying "thank you"

There are many ways to send a note of thanks: email, text, or the post office (remember "snail mail"?).

In the next two weeks send a note of thanks when someone in your life (family, friend, colleague, team member, etc.) has done something you appreciated. Be sure the note is genuine.

How did you feel while you were composing the note?

_____

_____

_____

How did you feel when it was delivered to them (by mail, in person, etc.)?

_____

_____

_____

Also note any reactions or responses from the person(s) who received the note. How did that make you feel?

_____

_____

_____

collectively

Activity 10: Find a Mentor

Goal: Identify mentors in different areas of your life

Make a list of the people that play a mentoring role in your life.

_____

_____

_____

Think about the other areas in your life that you want to grow and develop and identify people that could potentially serve in that area.

_____

_____

_____

Do your research about who that person is and brainstorm creative ways you can connect with that person- think of different ways to connect with that person because they may be really busy. For example, maybe you can join a group they are already a part of, or work on a committee together.

_____

_____

_____

Take time to do your homework to make sure that you have chosen the right person. Also try to identify what you can do for that person- remember the theory of reciprocity.

_____

_____

_____

Having a mentor/mentee relationship is mutually beneficial.

Activity 11: Take the Risk

Goal: Getting to know new people

Identify three people that you would like to get to know better. Be intentional and think about why you want to get to know them better (what can you do for them and what can they do for you).

_____

_____

_____

Identify what you can do together and what experiences you share.

_____

_____

_____

Send a text or email inviting them to connect.

Activity 12: Lean In On Those Who Challenge You

Goal: Connecting with someone who challenges you

Think for a moment about the people in your world that challenge you- either they push you to be better, or they push your buttons.

Try to identify what it is about that person that creates the most challenge.

_____

_____

_____

Why do you think that is such a challenge for you?

_____

_____

_____

How can you connect with that person to learn more about how you can grow in that space?

_____

_____

_____

Activity 13: Look Outside Your Inner Circle

Goal: Intentionally expand your inner circle

Take a moment and think about your inner circle.

Next identify 5 ways you can expand that circle.

_____

_____

_____

Where can you look for new connections?

_____

_____

_____

Look on social media under events; or ask three friends where they hear about community events.

_____

_____

_____

Think about what you enjoy and look for an activity in the community- attend even if you don't know anyone going.

_____

_____

_____

Identify what event you can attend this week that will help you continue looking outside of your inner circle.

_____

_____

_____

Activity 14: Asset Mapping Activity

Goal: Developing community supports

List several different organizations and groups that exist in your community. This could include formal organizations such as houses of worship, civic organizations, bowling leagues, motorcycle clubs, or rock star fan clubs.

_____

_____

_____

Select three groups and discuss how their missions or activities might provide reciprocal support for you.

_____

_____

_____

Select one of the identified groups and develop an action plan for how you could get them involved.

_____

_____

_____

Activity 15: Purpose in Life

Goal: Identify how your gifts and strengths can help solve a problem

Divide paper into three sections.

In the first section, list your gifts, strengths, talents, including abilities and personal qualities.

In the third section, list problems in the world that are concerning to you, such as child abuse, animal abuse, unemployment, etc.

In the middle section, use creativity to devise at least three ways to use your gifts in the first section to solve problems in the third section.

Draw and color an image of one of these ideas as if it has already happened and succeeded in solving the problem.

GIFTS, STRENGTHS, TALENTS, ABILITIES, QUALITIES	3 WAYS TO USE YOUR GIFTS	PROBLEMS IN THE WORLD

Activity 16: Getting Involved

Goal: Using your strengths, talents, and interests to get involved in your local community

Based on your strengths, interests and talents from the previous activity, research local non-profit organizations to identify how you can get involved.

Contact the organization or attend an event they are hosting to learn more and get involved.

What are your strengths, interests, and talents?

_____

_____

_____

Identify three local non-profits doing work in that space (three lines with contact numbers). Note for when you make the call.

Name   **Contact Information**

_____

_____

_____

Activity 17: Relationship Needs

Goal: Practice reciprocity

Select a magazine picture to represent you and glue it to the middle of a large piece of paper.

Select magazine pictures to represent the six most important people in your life and glue them in a circle around you.

Draw a line connecting each of the people to the picture of you.

On the top of each line, write a word or phrase about what you need from that person.

Under each line, write a word or phrase about what that person needs from you. Identify how you can support that need and practice reciprocity.

Activity 18: Tank of Gas

Goal: Identify how "full" your tank of gas is

Even with great talents, someone with low self-esteem can't get very far. It would be like having a nice car without any gas. On the other hand, some people who have physical limitations have achieved great things due to their self-confidence.

Make two columns on a piece of paper.

On one column, list the areas of your life that you feel confident about, and on the other column, list the areas of life that you feel insecure about; i.e. academics, work, appearance, creativity, making friends, etc.

Count the number of items listed in each column and write the total at the bottom of each list.

Subtract the Insecure total from the Confident total: that is how much gas you have left in your tank.

On another piece of paper, make a visual affirmation of your ability to improve your confidence and self-acceptance in areas of your life that you are currently insecure about.

Think about the people in your life or that you need to call into your life to help you fill your tank based on the areas of your life you feel insecure about.

CONFIDENT	INSECURE

Activity 19: Dream Team

Goal: Identify your "dream team"

In a school a dream team is a community of champions who rally around every child to help them reach their greatest potential. A "champion" is a close-knit network of people that can help support your goals, provide feedback on your goals, and work with you to hold you accountable for your goals. You meet with your "dream team" periodically to review your progress. A champion can be coaches, pastors/rabbis/imams, parents, friends, peers, and mentors, etc.

You can create your dream team too.

What is one goal you want to accomplish?

_____

_____

Who are your champions (list 3-4)?

_____

_____

_____

_____

Reach out to your champions and ask them if they will be willing to be on your dream team.

c⊛llectively

Activity 20: Transformational Action Plan

Goal: Using the activities, select two to improve your social capital

What change(s) are you going to make to improve your social capital?

AREA FOR GROWTH	
STRENGTHS RESOURCES	
ACTION STEPS	
WHO SUPPORTS GROWTH	
TIME FRAME	

Chapter 4 ~ Social Media

The next social influence of mental health is social media. When we learn to manage our social media intake, we have better mental health. Did you know that recent figures show 88.2% of the US population utilizes social media? Further, 90% of us actively engage with and contribute to multiple social media platforms. Unfortunately, research demonstrates that both adult and youth social media users report higher stress.

We've all been through a lot in the past few years and for many, social media has been a way to connect with others when we were not sure if we should connect in person. Clinical psychologist and social media expert, Ben Buchanan counsels people struggling to foster friendships, and says social media has helped some of them feel less isolated.

There is important research around the concept of strong ties and weak ties. In order to stay healthy, humans need three to five significant relationships. Strong ties are those three to five significant relationships, whereas weak ties are connections that we build through networking. Social media accounts for a platform to build weak ties. The danger is when we forsake real-world relationships for virtual friendships. Buchanan says research indicates those relationships of the highest quality, which last the longest, tend to be the ones where you see each other face to face.

So why is this so important?

According to the World Health Organization, depression and anxiety have increased by 25% in the past two years. While this is largely due to the pandemic, many of the changes were in motion prior to Covid and resulted in a lack of social connection. In the short term, the social media platform was useful and necessary, however, in the long term, continued heavy usage (more than 3 hours per day) results in the increased mental health conditions we are seeing today.

People often ask how does social media result in depression? While there are some obvious reasons like strong and weak ties, there are also some physiological reasons that we should be aware of. Not to get all sciency on you, but this is how social media impacts the brain.

The average person spends over 3 hours on their smart phone each day, including approximately two and a half hours on social media (have you tracked your usage lately?)

Research shows that doing anything repeatedly for extended amounts of time causes physiological changes in the brain. In fact, that's how habits form.

Social media does something called "capture and scatter" your attention; meaning when we hit refresh, constant new information enters your brain. Thus, you are constantly excited and rewarded to see new information and posts. This is why we reach for our phone to check our messages so frequently.

Studies show this ability to capture your attention is detrimental to your brain.

Heavy social media users perform worse on cognitive tests, lose their ability to multitask, need to exert more effort to stay focused, and actually lose memory. In fact, heavy social media use actually shrinks parts of the brain and effects the neuroplasticity of the brain.

Further, social media makes you addicted to your screens. It provides immediate rewards in the form of a dopamine release (the happy hormone) every time you post or get a notification from the app. Yay! New input, someone likes me!

This constant barrage of shallow rewards rewires your brain to want more of what caused that dopamine release, which leads to social media addiction. So, how many times a day are you checking your messages?

This also means that when your brain does not get the dopamine release, you experience sadness.

There are multiple studies looking at the brain and what social media usage looks like.

Did you know…. studies show that the brain scans of heavy social media users look very similar to those addicted to drugs or gambling. Further, those who use multiple social media platforms have substantially higher odds of having increased levels of both depression and anxiety symptoms (Primack, et.al, 2018). In fact, "the greater your level of Facebook addiction, the lower your brain volume. MRI brain scans of Facebook users demonstrated a significant reduction in gray matter in the amygdala correlated with their level of addiction to Facebook. The erosion of brain matter is similar to the type of cell death seen in cocaine addicts" (He, Turel & Bechara, 2017).

Ultimately, social media is here to stay so we need to find a way to balance the benefits and risks associated. Our world has become more accessible, and we can connect with people near and far. It's important to keep in mind that we need to focus on living in the tangible world as well as the virtual world. Having authentic connections with people will support better mental health. According to U.S. Surgeon General Vivek Murthy, "What often matters is not the quantity or frequency of social contact but the quality of our connections and how we feel about them".

Here are some activities you may use to assess, identify, and intentionally utilize social media to improve our mental health.

Activity 1: Screen Time Assessment

Goal: Identify your weekly amount of screen time

Look at your phone and under the settings there should be an option to look at your screen time. You can look at your daily usage or how much you looked at your phone in the past week. Take a moment to audit this information and answer the following questions:

Were you surprised with what you noticed?

_____

_____

_____

What did you expect and what did you see?

_____

_____

_____

Is this number acceptable to you? _____

If you looked at the weekly usage, multiply it by 52. Are you comfortable spending this number of hours/ days every year looking at your screen? (For example: If my usage was on average 4 hours per day or 28 hours per week.) 28 hours X 52 weeks = 1456 hours per year. If I then divide that by 24 hours in a day= 60 days. That means I'm spending 60 full days every year on social media. Do the math…are you ok with your number? _____

Think about what your acceptable number is: _____

What are some ways that you can lower your screen time? Think of some of the activities from previous chapters. Try it for a week and reflect on how you felt.

_____

_____

_____

_____

Activity 2: Social Media Assessment

Goal: Honestly assess your social media use

This survey is designed to provide a quick assessment of whether you might have problems with excessive use of social media. However, no test is 100% accurate. No matter what your score is, you should seek help from a health professional if you have any concerns about yourself or your loved ones.

The questionnaire used here is the Social Media Disorder (SMD) Scale by Dr. Regina van den Eijnden

Read each question below and answer each one honestly. Take a look at your response and decide if there is anything you would like to change about your social media habits.

During the past year, have you…

1. … regularly found that you can't think of anything else but the moment that you will be able to use social media again?
   ☐ yes   ☐ no

2. … regularly felt dissatisfied because you wanted to spend more time on social media?
   ☐ yes   ☐ no

3. … often felt bad when you could not use social media?
   ☐ yes   ☐ no

4. … regularly neglected other activities (e.g. hobbies, sport) because you wanted to use social media?
   ☐ yes   ☐ no

5. … regularly had arguments with others because of your social media use?
   ☐ yes   ☐ no

6. … regularly lied to family members or friends about the amount of time you spend on social media?
   ☐ yes   ☐ no

7. … often used social media to escape from negative feelings?
   ☐ yes   ☐ no

8. … had serious conflict with family members (e.g. parents, brother(s) or sister(s), spouse) because of your social media use?
   ☐ yes   ☐ no

Source: https://pure.uva.nl/ws/files/16231343/Social_Media_Disorder_Scale.pdf

Activity 3: Social Media Audit

Goal: Find out what you watch on social media

Let's audit what we watch on social media. When we spend time on social media we are literally allowing an algorithm to decide whom we connect with and what information we allow into our brains. It's important for us to be able to identify what is helpful and what is not.

Choose your favorite social media platform and set a timer for 5 minutes and begin scrolling.

On the page below, write down what posts you see and on a scale of 1-10 (10 being good), how do they make you feel. Taking an audit like this allows you to become aware of what you are ingesting. Interestingly, because social media gives you more of what you put out there or what you look for, taking a moment to become aware of what we are looking for is useful.

WHAT POSTS DID YOU SEE?	1-10

What did you notice?

Activity 4: Social Media Intention

Goal: Follow sites with intention

Now that you know what you are allowing into your brain, let's be intentional.

What did you come across that made you feel good compared to want made you feel bad.

List 5 sites that you will un-follow:

_____

_____

_____

_____

_____

Now, look for 5 new positive sites to replace the ones you deleted. List them out here:

_____

_____

_____

_____

_____

Set an intention to follow those sites for at least one week and see how your view changes.

Activity 5: Let's Make a Deal

Goal: Managing your social media time

People often report that social media is a distraction. They get frustrated with themselves when they procrastinate on a project only to find that they spent the 2 hours they were supposed to be working, mindlessly scrolling on social media.

One technique is to reward yourself with 30 minutes of social media after the completion of an important task. Now I'm not saying go walk the dog and then come back and reward yourself with 30 minutes on social. It should be a task that NEEDS to be completed like an assignment in school, a work project, or a larger than everyday chore.

Identify a project that needs to be completed today:

_____

_____

How much time on social media will be your reward when you complete the task

_____

_____

Go!

Activity 6: Active Social Media Usage

Goal: Using social media for positive connection and communication

There is research around the benefits of active social media usage (posting, commenting, and creating videos to post) as opposed to passive usage (just sitting and scrolling). Active usage is better for you because there is connection and communication.

Take time to create a post about mental health. It can be a video or reel, you can go on Canva and design it, just make it interactive with a call to action about something that the reader should need to do or comment on.

What's your post going to be about?

_____

_____

_____

_____

_____

Activity 7: Using Social Media Before You Meet People

Goal: Using social media to help with social anxiety

In business it is a common practice to research the people that you are meeting prior to meeting with them. We can do the same thing in our everyday lives. If you are making an effort to be more social or connect with others in person but have some anxiety around meeting new people, this is a great hack.

Say you are going to a networking event or getting together with someone you are meeting for the first time, looking them up in advance may make you feel more comfortable. Try to determine what their interests are so you have some ideas on what to talk about.

Identify the next time you have a planned meeting with someone new.

_____

What social media platform is best for that aged person?

_____

Go to that platform and document what you found our about that person.

_____

_____

_____

_____

_____

What topics of conversation will help you better connect with that person?

_____

_____

_____

_____

_____

Activity 8: Love Scrolling

Goal: Making positive comments

Take 5 minutes (set a timer) and scroll on your favorite platform. Every time you see something that makes you happy or smile, write a positive comment on that post. It could be "You rock". "Congratulations", or "I'm proud of you". At the end of 5 minutes, answer the questions below:

How many posts did you comment on? _____

Was this easy or difficult to write something positive? _____

How would you feel if someone commented on your post like that?

_____

_____

_____

How are you feeling right now?

_____

_____

_____

_____

_____

_____

_____

Activity 9: Reach Out and Connect

Goal: Using social media for positive connections

Take a moment and think of a person that makes you smile... choose your favorite platform (it could just be a text) and write them a positive message and send it...

Who did you reach out to? _____

What did you say?

_____

_____

What was their response?

_____

_____

If you're feeling lonely, look through your text or snap chat and identify three people that you would like to connect with. For each person, think about what they enjoy, and find a picture, article, song, around that topic. Send it to them with a message, "Made me think of you."

Who will you connect with? _____

What do they enjoy?

_____

What was their response?

_____

_____

How did you feel when they responded to you?

_____

_____

Did you feel less lonely? Why?

_____

_____

Activity 10: Common Interests

Goal: Using social media to connect with others that have common interests

Think about an interest that you have and search for an online forum to connect with people with common interests. Join groups that inspire you to be the person you want to be.

What are you interested in?

_____

What online groups can you connect with around that interest?

_____

_____

Can you identify a local event or activity around that same interest?

_____

_____

Who can you go to the local activity with?

_____

_____

Activity 11: It's All About the Energy

Goal: Understand the impact on the brain

Understanding how social media impacts our brain is important. When we see something we like, we get a rush of energy. That energy feels good so we want more of what we like. Then, when we stop seeing what we like, our brain doesn't send that energy, so we feel sad. That makes us miss the good feeling, so we go back for more. If we want to get away from social media, we need to identify what makes us feel good off-line.

Identify 10 things that you really enjoy doing and gives you that rush of energy (in person):

1. _____

2. _____

3. _____

4. _____

5. _____

6. _____

7. _____

8. _____

9. _____

10. _____

How can you begin to incorporate these activities into your life as a positive replacement behavior for social media?

_____

_____

_____

_____

_____

_____

Activity 12: Social Media Habit Scroll

Goal: Identify what makes you scroll

We have already identified how much as well as what we like to follow on social media. Now let's pay attention to what makes us want to start scrolling.

We call these triggers and it means that something is making us want to do a certain behavior. Perhaps we are bored, perhaps our friends are online at a particular time, and perhaps we're trying to avoid something in our external world. Identify the reasons that you reach for social media.

What time of day?

_____
_____
_____
_____
_____

What is happening that makes you want to escape?

_____
_____
_____
_____

What are potential triggers that you can avoid if you want to change how much or when you reach for social?

_____
_____
_____
_____
_____

Activity 13: The Social Dilemma

Goal: Learning the impact of social media

If you're curious about how social media is impacting us all, scan the QR code below to watch the movie "The Social Dilemma."

What were your takeaways?

_____

_____

_____

_____

_____

Name one thing that you will do differently since watching the movie.

_____

_____

Activity 14: Fear of Missing Out

Goal: Changing your mindset from FOMO to JOMO

FOMO or "Fear of Missing Out" is a real thing. Many people report that they scroll on social media to see what others are up to, and then sometimes we find that we were not included in the activities that people we know are enjoying.

The struggle is real.

There is research about changing our mindset from FOMO to JOMO ("Joy Of Missing Out"). When you find that others are doing something that you are not, look around at what you have, recognize why your current situation or space is just where you need to be now.

Take a moment right now to intentionally look around you and identify 10 things that you are grateful for.

_____

_____

_____

_____

_____

_____

_____

_____

_____

Next time you are online and experience FOMO, use this technique to appreciate what is around you or ways that you can make changes to your space to make it even more comfortable.

Activity 15: Boundaries

Goal: Create social media rules

Create some rules for yourself around social media. If you are trying to improve your mental health and social media is one of your action steps, what are your non-negotiables? Here are some examples:

No social media during meals- make the table a sacred space to connect with the people in your life.

Stop looking at social media 1 hour before bed to ensure that you get the best night sleep.

Don't look at social media when you are spending time with friends (or allow yourselves 5 minute social media check ins).

What are your non-negotiables? (list 3 to 5)

_____

_____

_____

_____

_____

Activity 16: It's Time for Vacay

Goal: Taking a break from your phone

Take a break from the phone. Choose a day per week that you will leave the phone off.

You don't have to leave it at home if you're worried about safety, just turn it off for the day.

What are your fears about turning your phone off, worst-case scenario about not being connected to your phone?

_____

_____

_____

What would happen if you responded one day later to a post, text, or call?

_____

_____

_____

Reflection:

How did it feel not being connected to your device during the day?

_____

_____

_____

As you reflect on the day, what did you notice?

_____

_____

_____

Activity 17: Making Connections

Goal: Meeting new people and fostering the connection

When you meet someone new, do you connect online? This is a great way to nurture new connections and build potential connections. It's best to connect while you are meeting them or right after you have met. When doing this, only connect with someone you trust. It's okay to connect online with someone new, but don't share personal information (phone number or address) unless you get to know them better.

Think of the last 5 new people that you met

_____

_____

_____

_____

_____

Did you connect with them online?

_____

_____

_____

Activity 18: Gratitude and Your Brain

Goal: Take a gratitude challenge

Take the 7 Day Live Happy Gratitude Challenge- Every day answer the questions and create a post on social media with your results.

Day 1-Think of two challenges you're grateful for and what positive things you learned?

_____

_____

Day 2- What skills are you grateful to have?

_____

Day 3- If you had a positive experience at a store or business, shout it out on social.

_____

Day 4- What foods are you thankful for? Can you share that food with someone?

_____

Day 5- Think of three memories you're most thankful for. If someone else is involved, send them a note.

_____

_____

_____

Day 6- What exercise are you most thankful that you are able to do?

_____

Day 7- Think about the material comforts that you're grateful for- make as long of a list as you can.

_____

What kind of comments did you get from your posts during the week?

_____

How did the comments make you feel?

_____

Source: https://livehappy.com/practice/7-day-gratitude-challenge

Activity 19: Positive Messaging

Goal: Share a positive message

Intentionally use your social media to share positive messages. When we project out positivity, it comes back to us. The sites below are great for quotes and potential social media posts:

passiton.com/inspirational-quotes

morninglazziness.com/quotes/social-media-quotes/

realsimple.com/work-life/life-strategies/inspiration-motivation/positive-quotes

Activity 20: Transformational Action Plan

Goal: Using the activities, create an action plan

Based on the activities, create an action plan for how you want to manage your social media to improve your mental health. Take into account your current usage and your ideal usage. Also, think about the activities online that are better for your mental health and incorporate them into your plan. Write your plan out.

AREA FOR GROWTH	
STRENGTHS RESOURCES	
ACTION STEPS	
WHO SUPPORTS GROWTH	
TIME FRAME	

Chapter 5 ~ Social Inclusion

Another aspect of the Social Influences of Mental Health is Social Inclusion. Social Inclusion is the process by which efforts are made to ensure equal opportunities—that everyone, regardless of their background, can achieve their full potential in life. A socially inclusive society is one where all groups have a sense of belonging, participation, recognition and legitimacy. Social inclusiveness respects diversity and actually seeks diversity. In this world, we all deserve to have access to the same opportunities to be happy and healthy.

Sadly, there are barriers to all groups being able to fully participate in political, economic, and social life globally. The disadvantage is often based on **gender, age, location, occupation, race, ethnicity, religion, citizenship status, disability, and sexual orientation and gender identity (SOGI)**, among other factors. This kind of social exclusion robs individuals of dignity, security, and the opportunity to lead a better life.

Social inclusion involves the behavior and treatment in terms of the distribution of wealth, opportunities and privileges within a society and equal rights and equitable opportunities for all. Social inclusion requires living the principles and values and seeking ways to embody them in everything we do. It requires change at multiple levels among many people and can be messy and uncomfortable.

Like the other Social Influences of Mental Health, our everyday actions impact our level of happiness. There is extensive research around how altruism improves our mental health. If we live the values of social inclusion and intentionally work to help those less fortunate, it improves both their lives as well as our mental health. Living a life of purpose and focusing on the greater good has proven benefits to both society as well as ourselves.

In this chapter we will explore ways to understand ourselves and our purpose as well as how we can live a more inclusive life.

Activity 1: Identifying My Purpose

Goal: Getting to know myself- to understand how I can contribute to society

List two of your unique personal qualities, such as enthusiasm and creativity.

_____

_____

List one or two ways you enjoy expressing those qualities when interacting with others, such as support and inspire.

_____

_____

Assume the world is perfect right now. What does this world look like? How is everyone interacting with everyone else? What does it feel like? Write your answer as a statement, in the present tense, describing the ultimate condition, the perfect world as you see it and feel it. Remember, a perfect world is a fun place to be.

EXAMPLE: _Everyone is freely expressing their own unique talents. Everyone is working in harmony. Everyone is expressing love._

_____

_____

Combine the three prior subdivisions of this paragraph into a single statement.

EXAMPLE: My purpose is to use my creativity and enthusiasm to support and inspire others to freely express their own talents in a harmonious and loving way.

_____

_____

_____

_____

Activity 2: Being Proud of Myself

Goal: Self-awareness of how our characteristics can be seen as both positive and negative

On one side of your paper, list the following: age, race, body type, speech/ language, fashion/ style, mental ability, physical ability, sexual orientation, social style, income/ financial.

Make two columns entitled: Advantage and Disadvantage. Place a check in one or both of the columns for each word depending on whether that characteristic has been an advantage or disadvantage in your life. For example, a teen might say his age is both a disadvantage and an advantage because people treat him like a child and he's not allowed to drive, but he also isn't responsible for bills or working and can still have fun.

	ADVANTAGE	DISADVANTAGE
Age		
Race		
Body Type		
Speech/Language		
Fashion/Style		
Mental Ability		
Physical Ability		
Sexual Orientation		
Social Style		
Income/Financial		

Activity 3: Law Books

Goal: Understanding motivation for the way we act

Review Kohlberg's six stages of morality

KOHLBERG'S THEORY OF MORAL DEVELOPMENT

EXPLANATION

Kohlberg devised a theory of moral development which postulates that moral reasoning passes through six stages from early childhood to adulthood.

Kohlberg's stages are sorted into three levels: preconventional morality, conventional morality, and post-conventional morality.

Each stage involves a more advanced level of reasoning that coincides with cognitive development and life experiences.

STAGES

Obedience/Punishment Orientation

Individualism and Exchange

Establishing Interpersonal Relationships

Maintaining Social Order

Social Contract and Individual Rights

Universal Principles

Do you do the right thing to:

1. Avoid punishment?
2. Gain reward?
3. Be regarded as a good person?
4. Because you believe in the law?
5. Because you believe in a social contract?
6. Because you feel what is right and wrong in your own heart?

Make a book of laws as you would like them to be, including one page each for the following topics: World Laws, Society Laws, School Laws, Friendship Laws, Romantic Relationship Laws, Family Laws, and Self Laws.

Source: https://helpfulprofessor.com/kohlbergs-theory-of-moral-development/

Activity 4: Educate Yourself About Social Inclusion Issues

Goal: Using your interests to make a difference in your community

Navigating how to get involved can be overwhelming. The best way to start is to familiarize yourself with social issues that you're passionate about and research what is being done about them. Whether it's hunger and food insecurity, gun violence, voting rights, or another issue, you'll gain a better understanding of an issue's current state by learning about its history.

What three social inclusion issues are you passionate about?

_____

_____

_____

Choose one that is most important _____

Research local groups that are working on this issue, what did you find?

_____

_____

_____

Reach out to learn more. How can you get involved?

_____

_____

_____

_____

_____

Activity 5: Four Elements of You

Goal: Know Thyself

Passion gives us the will to live and gives shape to our lives. Knowing yourself will help you identify your values and how you will show up in this world.

Fold your paper into four sections. Label each section: The Earth of Me, The Air of Me, The Fire of Me, and The Water of Me. Use image and color to express your passion in life as symbolized by the four elements.

The Earth of Me	The Air of Me

The Fire of Me	The Water of Me

Activity 6: Self-Portraits

Goal: Exploring Our Appearance

Creating self-portraits is an opportunity to reflect on the physical aspects of our identity. Use paint, markers, colored pencils or crayons, to create individual or family portraits. Make sure your art supplies reflect the variety of colors, shades and complexions that represent a diversity of people. Before creating your self-portraits, think about different aspects of our physical identity. You might concentrate on your faces or look at your faces and bodies together. Look in the mirror and identify the shape of your face; skin color and complexion; eye shape and color; hair color, texture, length and style; nose shape; and other characteristics like birthmarks, freckles, glasses, braces, etc. Then make your self-portraits using all the information you just gathered

Discussion Prompts:

What do you notice about your self-portrait?

_____

_____

_____

How does your self-portrait reflect aspects of your identity in terms of race, ethnicity and other identity characteristics?

_____

_____

_____

How do you look similar to and different from people in your family, friends and classmates?

_____

_____

_____

Activity 7: Symbols of Respect & Inclusion

Goal: Recognize how symbols make people feel included or excluded

We see symbols every day—they are all around on buildings, in the street, on schoolyards, on our phones and in digital spaces. Symbols convey ideas, qualities, feelings, objects, opinions and beliefs. Unfortunately, symbols are also used to spread bias and hate. Explore the idea that symbols can be positive, neutral, or negative. Brainstorm symbols that express positive values and concepts such as respect, diversity, inclusion, love, acceptance and friendship.

Answer these questions:

Why are symbols important?

_____

_____

_____

What symbols have you noticed and are they positive, negative or neutral?

_____

_____

_____

How can symbols of respect and inclusion make a difference in your community and the larger society?

_____

_____

_____

Activity 8: Examine Your Beliefs and Habits

Goal: Understanding why we believe the way we believe about others

Many of us hold onto beliefs that we learned as children, and they can influence how we engage in society. Positive action toward inclusion and advocacy begins at home. Becoming a strong ally of social inclusion requires ongoing self-reflection, learning, and openness to growth. Reflect on what you were taught as a child about the following:

A person living on the street without a home

_____

_____

Someone who is blind

_____

_____

A person from another country that doesn't have a place to live

_____

_____

Someone who used to be in armed service

_____

_____

Someone who looks different than you based on skin color

_____

_____

Someone who is a different gender

_____

_____

Someone who is elderly

_____

Activity 9: I Am...I Am Not

Goal: Examining stereotypes about ourselves

List three identifying qualities about yourself and then identify three of the potential stereotypes that you think of related to those stereotypes.

I am *tall* but I am not a *basketball player*

I am _____ but I am not _____

I am _____ but I am not _____

I am _____ but I am not _____

Activity 10: Butterfly Initiation

Goal: Learn about how other cultures see the life cycle

Discuss with someone or research on your own initiation rites of indigenous cultures that enacted a death/ rebirth cycle for youth. Compare that process to the death and rebirth of a butterfly larvae entering a cocoon phase in which its body disintegrates before forming the adult butterfly.

Divide paper into four segments and label each one; Child, Preparation, Death, and Rebirth.

Draw, color, or paint an artistic representation in each box, such as caterpillar, cocoon weaving, disintegration in the cocoon, and the butterfly.

Child	Preparation

Death	Rebirth

Activity 11: Compliment Tags

Goal: Recognize that all people can posses positive inner qualities

Examples of compliments:

I love hanging out with you!

You are kind!

You have a great sense of humor!

My day is better with you in it!

You are a good friend!

You are brave!

Compliment someone not based on appearance. Here are some ideas to help you get started.

Identify three people you will compliment:

What will you compliment them about?

Name: _____ compliment: _____

Name: _____ compliment: _____

Name: _____ compliment: _____

Reflection:

How did the person react?

_____

_____

_____

How did it feel to compliment someone not based on their appearance?

_____

_____

_____

Activity 12: What Does it Mean to be Resilient

Goal: Understanding how we overcome challenges helps us to have empathy for others

Everyone faces adversity in life. But imagination and creativity support resilience, helping individuals transform life's most challenging obstacles into opportunities for self-awareness and self-expression.

Watch the following 10-minute film:

https://www.globalonenessproject.org/library/films/everything-incredible

Reflection:

The title of the film is taken from Agustin's statement, "The problem is that everything is incredible and people don't accept it." What do you think Agustin means by this statement?

_____

_____

_____

_____

_____

Think of a time when you have felt broken down by the world; how did you find resiliency to move past it?

_____

_____

_____

_____

_____

Source: https://www.globalonenessproject.org/library/films/everything-incredible

Activity 13: How Food Can be Inclusive

Goal: Understand how others from different cultures celebrate holidays

Think about your favorite meal and answer the following questions:

What is the meal? _____

_____

Who makes the meal? _____

_____

What are the ingredients? _____

_____

What are the rituals when you eat it? (day, time, prayer/thanks...) _____

_____

_____

Who do you usually share it with? _____

_____

_____

With a group of friends, ask each person to describe their favorite meal.

_____

_____

_____

_____

_____

_____

_____

_____

_____

Activity 14: Picture Exchange

Goal: Learn from others what makes them feel included

Look at pictures and identify a time when you felt included and part of a group or community.

Ask three friends to look in their pictures and share a time when they felt included as part of a community.

Who will you ask:

_____

_____

_____

What did they say?

_____

_____

_____

_____

_____

_____

_____

_____

_____

Activity 15: Diversity Calendar

Goal: Understand holidays that you don't currently celebrate

Identify five holidays that you have never celebrated before and learn about them.

1. Holiday: _____

_____

_____

_____

2. Holiday: _____

_____

_____

_____

3. Holiday: _____

_____

_____

_____

4. Holiday: _____

_____

_____

_____

5. Holiday: _____

_____

_____

_____

Activity 16: Speak Your Truth

Goal: Build connection through honest conversation about inclusion

Identify someone to have an honest conversation with about inclusion and discrimination. You can tell them you are working on a project for a book that you are reading and you thought of them for this activity.

Before you begin the conversation, answer the following questions:

Have you ever felt discriminated against? What happened?

_____

_____

_____

_____

What actions would you take if you noticed someone being discriminated against?

_____

_____

_____

_____

What practices would you put in place to make sure that people feel included in the future?

_____

_____

_____

_____

Now have a conversation with the other person to share your findings and ask them to share theirs.

Activity 17: Inclusion-Driven Brand Support

Goal: Become aware of the brands that support inclusion for all

Research popular brands that practice inclusion by going on the internet and looking for inclusion statements.

Identify 5 brands and what they stand for:

1. Brand: _____

_____

2. Brand: _____

_____

3. Brand: _____

_____

4. Brand: _____

_____

5. Brand: _____

_____

What did you notice from your search?

_____

_____

_____

Are you more likely to purchase those products given a choice moving forward?

_____

Who will you share this information with?

_____

_____

_____

Activity 18: Inclusion Pledge

Goal: Recognize how stereotypes make people feel excluded and vow to be inclusive moving forward

Make a list of all the names that describe someone for being different.

_____

_____

_____

_____

_____

What do you notice about the words you just wrote? Are they positive or negative?

_____

_____

_____

_____

_____

Write your pledge to disavow the words.

Make your own pledge. Here are some words to get you started but feel free to make your own pledge:

"No one has the right to call me these names and I don't have the right to call anyone else these names. I pledge that I will accept others the way they are and try to appreciate people who are different from me. Most people act as they do based on their life experiences. I can ask them about their experiences to understand why they approach life the way that they do. If I really don't like someone, I will give them space to be who they are, and I will defend my right to be who I am. I can always choose to walk away from someone if I don't agree with how they are acting. (Add your own words)

Signed, _____ "

Activity 19: If I Ruled the World

Goal: Identify what changes you would make in this world around inclusion if you could

Think about three real life changes you would make to be more inclusive. This could be in your home, in your school, or your place of work.

What are your three changes and how would they result in more inclusivity?

1. Life Change: _____

_____

_____

_____

2. Life Change: _____

_____

_____

_____

3. Life Change: _____

_____

_____

_____

Who could you share this list with in order to make that space more inclusive?

_____

_____

_____

_____

_____

_____

Activity 20: Transformational Action Plan

Goal: Using the activities, select 2 to improve your social inclusion

What change(s) are you going to make to improve your social inclusion? Based on what you learned about yourself, what local community groups will you get involved with to continues building connections in an inclusive way?

AREA FOR GROWTH	
STRENGTHS RESOURCES	
ACTION STEPS	
WHO SUPPORTS GROWTH	
TIME FRAME	

c⊙llectively

"Do the best you can until you know better. Then when you know better, do better."

–May Angelou

Resources

Introduction

who.int/news/item/27-08-2020-world-mental-health-day-an-opportunity-to-kick-start-a-massive-scale-up-in-investment-in-mental-health

cdc.gov/mentalhealth/learn/index.htm

vox.com/the-highlight/23402638/mental-health-psychiatrist-shortage-community-care-africa

dana.org/article/in-sync-how-humans-are-hard-wired-for-social-relationships/

brenebrown.com/book/atlas-of-the-heart/

greatergood.berkeley.edu/quizzes/take_quiz/social_capital

Social Connections

cnbc.com/2023/02/10/85-year-harvard-study-found-the-secret-to-a-long-happy-and-successful-life.html

Cacioppo, J. T., & Patrick, W. (2008). Loneliness: Human nature and the need for social connection. W W Norton & Co.

cdc.gov/nchs/index.htm

cssp.org/our-work/projects/protective-factors-framework/

ottawapublichealth.ca/en/public-health-services/have-that-talk.aspx

hello4health.org/

youtube.com/watch?v=8az-gfIjEbg

dailymail.co.uk/health/article-1265548/Smiling-add-years-life.html

Social Support

Luthar SS, Cicchetti D. The construct of resilience: implications for interventions and social policies. Dev Psychopathol. 2000 Autumn;12(4):857-85. doi: 10.1017/s0954579400004156. PMID: 11202047; PMCID: PMC1903337.

brenebrown.com/book/atlas-of-the-heart/

rand.org/pubs/research_reports/RR1875.html

musixmatch.com/

- Songwriters: Bill Withers. Lean on Me lyrics © Songs Of Universal Inc. - youtu.be/Nx_D0VTHBag

- Deloitte Meaningful connections Empowered Wellbeing material

Wintz, S., & Cooper, E. (2000-2003). Learning module cultural and spiritual sensitivity: A quick guide to cultures and spiritual traditions. Retrieved from the Association of Professional Chaplains: professionalchaplains.org/uploadedfiles/

taproot.com/live-your-core-values-exercise-to-increase-your-success/

aconsciousrethink.com/7171/qualities-good-friend/

bustle.com/life/qualities-of-a-good-friend

Social Capital

healthyplacesbydesign.org/

journals.uchicago.edu/doi/abs/10.1086/225469-strong%20ties-weak%20ties

socialcapitalresearch.com/

who.int/initiatives/sports-and-health/friendship-benches

sidewalk-talk.org/

Dmitri Williams, a professor at the University of Illinois, Urbana-Champaign

Williams, D. (2006). "On and Off the 'Net: Scales for Social Capital in an Online Era." Journal of Computer-Mediated Communication, 11, 593–628.

greatergood.berkeley.edu/quizzes/take_quiz/social_capital

youtube.com/watch?v=u9iK_nKrsc8

youtube.com/watch?v=tTvbf1WVYFE

Bettertogether: Conclusion – Changing the Wind – 100 Things You Can Do 1 Saguaro Seminar on Civic Engagement in America. John F. Kennedy School of Government, Harvard University, 79 JFK St., Cambridge, MA 02138 bettertogether.org

verywellmind.com/what-is-the-rule-of-reciprocity-2795891#:~:text=The%20reciprocity%20norm%20operates%20on,people%20do%20favors%20for%20them

blogs.scientificamerican.com/psysociety/i-8217-ll-show-you-my-holiday-card-if-you-show-me-yours/

Platonic: How the Science of Attachment Can Help You Make-and Keep- Friends by Dr. Marisa G. Franco

hundred.org/en/innovations/dream-teams-for-every-student#d12c4a35

Social Media

benbuchanan.com.au/2014/12/04/how-phone-habits-and-social-media-drain-our-brain/

Shensa A, Sidani JE, Dew MA, Escobar-Viera CG, Primack BA. Social Media Use and Depression and Anxiety Symptoms: A Cluster Analysis. Am J Health Behav. 2018 Mar 1;42(2):116-128. doi: 10.5993/AJHB.42.2.11. PMID: 29458520; PMCID: PMC5904786

Turel, O., Mouttapa, M. & Donato, E. Preventing problematic Internet use through video-based interventions: a theoretical model and empirical test. Behaviour & Information Technology 34, 349–362, doi :10.1080/0144929x.2014.936041 (2015).

hhs.gov/sites/default/files/surgeon-general-youth-mental-health-advisory.pdf

ementalhealth.ca/index.php?m=printSurvey&hideFormatting=1&ID=56

thesocialdilemma.com/

psychologytoday.com/us/blog/happiness-is-state-mind/201807/jomo-the-joy-missing-out

The Social Media Disorder (SMD) Scale by Dr. Regina van den Eijnden

- passiton.com/inspirational-quotes
- morninglazziness.com/quotes/social-media-quotes/
- realsimple.com/work-life/life-strategies/inspiration-motivation/positive-quotes

Social Inclusion

The Success Principles, written by Jack Canfield, who took it from Arnold MPatent, spiritual coach and author of You Can Have it All. His website is arnoldpatent.com

Kohlberg's six stages of morality – helpfulprofessor.com

adl.org/resources/tools-and-strategies/thinking-about-social-justice-through-crafts-and-conversation

educationonline.ku.edu/community/15-ways-to-advance-social-justice

weareteachers.com/social-justice-lesson-plans-resources/

globalonenessproject.org/lessons/what-does-it-mean-be-resilient

Made in the USA
Las Vegas, NV
26 July 2024

92981090R00083